Qualifications and Credit Framework (QCF)
AQ2013

LEVEL 2 CERTIFICATE IN ACCOUNTING

(QCF)

QUESTION BANK

Basic Costing

2013 Edition

First June 2013


ISBN 9781 4727 0345 3


*British Library Cataloguing-in-Publication Data*
A catalogue record for this book is available from the British Library


Published by

BPP Learning Media Ltd
BPP House
Aldine Place
London W12 8AA


www.bpp.com/learningmedia


Printed in the United Kingdom by **Martins of Berwick**
Sea View Works
Spittal
Berwick-Upon-Tweed
TD15 1RS

We are grateful to the AAT for permission to reproduce the AAT sample assessment(s). The answers to the AAT sample assessment(s) have been published by the AAT. All other answers have been prepared by BPP Learning Media Ltd.

# CONTENTS

Introduction                                          v

**Question and answer bank**

**Chapter tasks**                          **Questions**     **Answers**

| | | Questions | Answers |
|---|---|---|---|
| 1 | Introduction to basic costing systems | 3 | 39 |
| 2 | Elements of cost | 8 | 43 |
| 3 | Cost behaviour | 14 | 48 |
| 4 | Inventory classification and valuation | 19 | 52 |
| 5 | Classifying labour costs | 23 | 55 |
| 6 | Coding costs | 27 | 57 |
| 7 | Comparison of costs and income | 31 | 59 |
| AAT AQ2013 Sample Assessment | | 65 | 81 |
| BPP practice assessment 1 | | 97 | 115 |
| BPP practice assessment 2 | | 129 | 147 |
| BPP practice assessment 3 | | 161 | 177 |
| BPP practice assessment 4 | | 189 | 207 |
| BPP practice assessment 5 | | 221 | 239 |
| BPP practice assessment 6 | | 253 | 271 |

# INTRODUCTION

This is BPP Learning Media's AAT Question Bank for Basic Costing. It is part of a suite of ground-breaking resources produced by BPP Learning Media for the AAT's assessments under the Qualification and Credit Framework.

Basic Costing is computer assessed. As well as being available in the traditional paper format, this **Question Bank is available in an online environment** containing tasks similar to those you will encounter in the AAT's testing environment. BPP Learning Media believe that the best way to practise for an online assessment is in an online environment. However, if you are unable to practise in the online environment you will find that all tasks in the paper Question Bank have been written in a style that is as close as possible to the style that you will be presented with in your online assessment.

This Question Bank has been written in conjunction with the BPP Text, and has been carefully designed to enable students to practise all of the learning outcomes and assessment criteria for the units that make up Basic Costing. It is fully up to date as at June 2013 and reflects both the AAT's unit guide and the sample assessment provided by the AAT.

This Question Bank contains these key features:

- tasks corresponding to each chapter of the Text. Some tasks are designed for learning purposes, others are of assessment standard

- the AAT's sample assessment and answers for Basic Costing and further BPP practice assessments

The emphasis in all tasks and assessments is on the practical application of the skills acquired.

## VAT

You may find tasks throughout this Question Bank that need you to calculate or be aware of a rate of VAT. This is stated at 20% in these examples and questions.

## Approaching the assessment

When you sit the assessment it is very important that you follow the on screen instructions. This means you need to carefully read the instructions, both on the introduction screens and during specific tasks.

When you access the assessment you should be presented with an introductory screen with information similar to that shown below (taken from the introductory screen from the AAT's AQ2013 Sample Assessment for Basic Costing).

The actual instructions will vary depending on the subject you are studying for. It is very important you read the instructions on the introductory screen and apply them in the assessment. You don't want to lose marks when you know the correct answer just because you have not entered it in the right format.

In general, the rules set out in the AAT sample assessment for the subject you are studying for will apply in the real assessment, but you should again read the information on this screen in the real assessment carefully just to make sure. This screen may also confirm the VAT rate used if applicable.

A full stop is needed to indicate a decimal point. We would recommend using minus signs to indicate negative numbers and leaving out the comma signs to indicate thousands, as this results in a lower number of key strokes and less margin for error when working under time pressure. Having said that, you can use whatever is easiest for you as long as you operate within the rules set out for your particular assessment.

You should complete all of the tasks. Don't leave questions unanswered.

In some assessments written or complex tasks may be human marked. In this case you are given a blank space or table to enter your answer into. You are told in the assessments

which tasks these are (note: there may be none if all answers are marked by the computer).

If these involve calculations, it is a good idea to decide in advance how you are going to lay out your answers to such tasks by practising answering them on a Word document, and certainly you should try all such tasks in this Question bank and in the AAT's environment using the sample/practice assessments.

When asked to fill in tables, or gaps, never leave any blank even if you are unsure of the answer. Fill in your best estimate.

Note that for some assessments where there is a lot of scenario information or tables of data provided (eg tax tables), you may need to access these via 'pop-ups'. Instructions will be provided on how you can bring up the necessary data during the assessment.

Finally, take note of any task specific instructions once you are in the assessment. For example, you may be asked to enter a date in a certain format or to enter a number to a certain number of decimal places.

Remember you can practise the BPP questions in this Question bank in an online environment on our dedicated AAT Online page. On the same page is a link to the current AAT Sample Assessment as well.

If you have any comments about this book, please e-mail ianblackmore@bpp.com or write to Ian Blackmore, AAT Product Manager, BPP Learning Media Ltd, BPP House, Aldine Place, London W12 8AA.

# Question bank

# Basic Costing Question bank

## Chapter 1 Introduction to basic costing systems

### Task 1.1

**Look at the definitions below and match them to the correct term, putting a tick in the relevant column of the table below.**

| Definition | Cash transaction | Credit transaction |
|---|---|---|
| Transactions whereby payment is immediate | | |
| Transactions whereby payment is to be made at some future date | | |

### Task 1.2

**Look at the definitions below and match them to the correct term, putting a tick in the relevant column of the table below.**

| Definition | Assets | Liabilities |
|---|---|---|
| Amounts that the business owes | | |
| Amounts that the business owns | | |

### Task 1.3

**Look at the definitions below and match them to the correct term, putting a tick in the relevant column of the table below.**

| Definition | Management accounting system | Financial accounting system |
|---|---|---|
| Recording transactions of the organisation in the ledgers to prepare financial statements | | |
| Recording transactions of the organisation to provide useful information for management | | |

## Task 1.4

**Look at the definitions below and match them to the correct term, putting a tick in the relevant column of the table below.**

| Definition | Budgets | Cost centre | Variances |
|---|---|---|---|
| An area of the organisation for which costs are collected together for management accounting purposes | | | |
| Differences that arise when the actual results of the organisation differ from the budgeted results | | | |
| Plans of the organisation for the next year in terms of money and/or resources | | | |

## Task 1.5

**For each of the following activities, indicate whether it comes under planning, decision-making or control. Put a tick in the correct box.**

| Activity | Planning | Decision-making | Control |
|---|---|---|---|
| Whether to expand the business | | | |
| Budgeting how many products to produce | | | |
| Regular comparison of actual activities to plans and budgets | | | |
| Reporting variances | | | |
| Management preparing strategic and operational plans | | | |
| Management deciding which suppliers to use | | | |

## Task 1.6

Businesses can be set up in a variety of different ways.

**Match the description to the types of business by ticking the correct box.**

| Description | Sole trader | Partnership | Limited company |
|---|---|---|---|
| A group of individuals who trade together to make a profit | | | |
| A business where the owner trades in their own name | | | |
| The owners delegate the running of the business to managers | | | |

## Task 1.7

Businesses make capital or revenue transactions.

**Indicate whether the following transactions are capital or revenue by ticking the correct box.**

| Transaction | Capital | Revenue |
|---|---|---|
| Purchase of a motor car for the managing director in a printing business | | |
| Purchase of a motor car by a garage for resale | | |
| Payment of wages | | |
| Rent on a workshop | | |
| Extension works on a workshop | | |
| Office furniture for the managing director | | |

## Task 1.8

Businesses fall into different types based on the different industries in which they operate.

**Identify which industry sectors the following businesses come under, ticking the correct box.**

| Description | Manufacturing | Retail | Service |
|---|---|---|---|
| Accountants, lawyers and other businesses which don't manufacture or sell a physical product | | | |
| The business buys in raw materials for making goods | | | |
| The business buys in ready-made goods which it sells on | | | |

## Task 1.9

**What is the purpose of accounting?**

**Select the ONE correct answer from the alternatives listed by ticking the box.**

| Definition | |
|---|---|
| To make decisions based on the best available data | |
| To control resources | |
| To record and accurately classify the transactions of the business | |
| To find the money to fund the owner's lifestyle | |

## Task 1.10

The table below lists some of the characteristics of financial accounting and management accounting systems.

**Indicate two characteristics for each system by putting a tick in the relevant column of the table below.**

| Characteristic | Financial accounting system | Management accounting system |
|---|---|---|
| It supports managers in their control activities | | |
| In a company it enables the production of accounts in a format required by law | | |
| It provides information to assist in management decision making | | |
| It ensures that all transactions are correctly classified as relating to assets, liabilities, capital, income or expenses | | |

## *Chapter 2 Elements of Cost*

### Task 2.1

Lascaux Ltd makes mosaic tiles for kitchens and bathrooms.

**Classify the following costs by element (materials, labour or overheads) by putting a tick in the relevant column of the table below.**

| Cost | Materials | Labour | Overheads |
|---|---|---|---|
| Glaze for the mosaic tiles | | | |
| Gas charges for heating the workshop | | | |
| Employees mixing the glazes for the tiles | | | |
| Clay used in making the tiles | | | |

### Task 2.2

Carcassone Ltd has a bistro and wine shop.

**Classify the following costs by nature (direct or indirect) by putting a tick in the relevant column of the table below.**

| Cost | Direct | Indirect |
|---|---|---|
| Wine bought in from a wholesaler | | |
| Business rates for the bistro | | |
| Wages of waiters and waitresses | | |
| Salary of shop manager | | |

## Task 2.3

Lyon Ltd makes guitars.

**Classify the following costs by function (production, administration, selling and distribution, or finance) by putting a tick in the relevant column of the table below.**

| Cost | Production | Administration | Selling and Distribution | Finance |
|---|---|---|---|---|
| Purchase of strings for making guitars | | | | |
| Advertising the instruments in the city tourist information shop | | | | |
| Wages of the bookkeeper | | | | |
| Salaries of craftsmen making the instruments | | | | |
| Interest charged on business overdraft | | | | |

## Task 2.4

Lille Ltd makes bread, cakes and pies for restaurants and its own chain of shops.

**Classify the following costs by element (materials, labour or overheads) by putting a tick in the relevant column of the table below.**

| Cost | Material | Labour | Overheads |
|---|---|---|---|
| Wages of pastry cooks | | | |
| Salesperson's salary for the year | | | |
| Confectioner's cream used to fill the pies | | | |
| Gas charges for the ovens | | | |

## Task 2.5

**Read the descriptions of labour costs below and match them to the correct term by putting a tick in the correct box.**

| Description | Basic pay | Overtime | Bonus |
|---|---|---|---|
| Amount paid for ordinary hours of work | | | |
| Hours worked above the normal hours stated in the employment contract | | | |
| Additional income for working more efficiently | | | |

## Task 2.6

Look at the costs listed below and indicate their nature and whether they are direct or indirect by putting a tick in the correct box.

| Description of cost | Direct materials | Direct labour | Indirect materials | Indirect labour | Indirect expenses |
|---|---|---|---|---|---|
| Factory supervisor's wages | | | | | |
| Lubricant for machinery | | | | | |
| Leather used to make shoes | | | | | |
| Hairdresser in a hair salon | | | | | |
| Telephone rental for administration office | | | | | |

## Task 2.7

Some costs can be incurred for a specific cost centre and some may be incurred for a range of cost centres jointly.

Identify whether each of the following expenses is specific to a single cost centre or is joint, by ticking the relevant box.

| Expense | Specific | Joint |
|---|---|---|
| Repair of machinery used by one production line only | | |
| Rent of workshop housing three cost centres | | |
| Business rates for the workshop housing three cost centres | | |
| Stationery used by the administration and payroll departments | | |
| Photocopier used by the managing director's personal assistant only | | |

## Task 2.8

Businesses make capital and revenue transactions.

**Indicate whether the following transactions are capital or revenue by ticking the correct box.**

| Transaction | Capital | Revenue |
|---|---|---|
| Installation of new machinery | | |
| Breakdown repairs on a faulty machine | | |
| Fees of bookkeeper | | |
| Purchase of new car for salesperson | | |

## Task 2.9

Trindle Sewing Machines makes sewing machines. The business has recently received invoices for the following expenses:

| | |
|---|---|
| Workshop rent | £4,500 |
| Warehouse rent | £2,500 |
| Office building rent | £1,000 |
| Safety testing of the assembly department | £400 |
| Overhaul of the grinding machines | £750 |
| Training for salesperson | £500 |

The workshop houses five departments, with the following approximate percentage of floor space:

| | |
|---|---|
| Grinding | 30% |
| Assembly | 25% |
| Testing | 15% |
| Security | 10% |
| Canteen | 20% |

The warehouse holds the stores and despatch departments, and the stores use approximately 70% of this area.

The office building contains the sales department (one cost centre) and administration, each using equal amounts of space.

Calculate the expenses to be collected for each of the cost centres and insert them in the table below. Show your working in your answer.

| Cost centre expense | Working | £ |
|---|---|---|
| Grinding – rent | | |
| Grinding – overhaul | | |
| Total Grinding | | |
| Assembly – rent | | |
| Assembly – safety testing | | |
| Total Assembly | | |
| Testing – rent | | |
| Despatch – rent | | |
| Stores – rent | | |
| Security – rent | | |
| Sales – rent | | |
| Sales – training | | |
| Total Sales | | |
| Canteen – rent | | |
| Administration – rent | | |

## Task 2.10

For a provider of car insurance, classify the following costs by element (materials, labour or overheads) by putting a tick in the relevant column of the table below.

| Cost | Materials | Labour | Overheads |
|---|---|---|---|
| Telephone costs for call centre | | | |
| Rent on call centre building | | | |
| Printer paper used for certificates of insurance sent to clients | | | |
| Salaries of client advisers | | | |

## Task 2.11

For a taxi firm, classify the following costs by nature (direct or indirect) by putting a tick in the relevant column of the table below.

| Cost | Direct | Indirect |
|---|---|---|
| Rent of booking office | | |
| Diesel for taxis | | |
| Wages of taxi drivers | | |
| Licence for firm from taxi regulator | | |

## Test 2.12

For a supplier of sandwiches to petrol station forecourts, classify the following costs by function (production, administration, or selling and distribution) by putting a tick in the relevant column of the table below.

| Cost | Production | Administration | Selling and Distribution |
|---|---|---|---|
| Wages of workers making sandwiches | | | |
| Fee for website maintenance | | | |
| Purchases of bread | | | |
| Fuel for delivery vehicle | | | |

# Chapter 3 Cost behaviour

## Task 3.1

Berlin Ltd makes stationery.

**Look at the costs below and classify them into variable, semi-variable, and fixed costs. Place a tick in the correct box.**

| Cost | Variable | Semi-variable | Fixed |
|---|---|---|---|
| Employee paid a basic wage plus commission based on production quantity | | | |
| Rent of the factory workshop | | | |
| Print ink used for letterheads and logos | | | |

## Task 3.2

Hamburg Ltd processes sausages and other meat products. It has a factory, warehouse and shop which sells the products.

**Look at the costs below and match them to the correct cost centre or profit centre by placing a tick in the relevant box.**

| Cost | Production cost centre | Service cost centre | Profit centre |
|---|---|---|---|
| Selling and marketing the products in the retail shop | | | |
| Mixing, filling and packing the sausages | | | |
| Storage in freezers in the warehouse | | | |

## Task 3.3

Baden is an accountancy partnership with several offices. Recently the partners decided to set up cost centres to run the partnership better.

**Look at the costs below and indicate which cost centre each would be collected under by placing a tick in the relevant box.**

| Cost | Audit | Tax | Personnel |
|------|-------|-----|-----------|
| Payroll software for paying salaries and wages | | | |
| Annual purchase of software updated for the year's Finance Act for the tax advisors | | | |
| Subscription to an audit advice helpline | | | |

## Task 3.4

**Look at the statements below and decide whether they are True or False by placing a tick in the correct box.**

| Cost | True | False |
|------|------|-------|
| Many fixed costs are only fixed over a certain range of output | | |
| Variable cost per unit falls as output rises | | |
| Direct costs are generally variable | | |
| Fixed cost per unit rises as output rises | | |

## Task 3.5

**Look at the statements below and decide whether they are True or False by placing a tick in the correct box.**

| Cost | True | False |
|------|------|-------|
| In a service organisation the Human Resources department is likely to be classified as a cost centre | | |
| Distribution would not be a cost centre in a manufacturing organisation | | |
| Stores could be a cost centre in a manufacturing or a service organisation | | |

## Task 3.6

Munich Ltd makes outdoor gym equipment. It incurs fixed costs of £50,000 per year in relation to the manufacture of its outdoor treadmills.

**Calculate the fixed cost per treadmill at each of the following four output levels and put your answers in the table below.**

| Output level of treadmills | Fixed cost per treadmill £ |
|:---:|:---:|
| 1,000 | |
| 10,000 | |
| 25,000 | |
| 100,000 | |

## Task 3.7

Munich Ltd also incurs £35 per treadmill for variable costs in manufacturing the treadmills.

**Calculate the total variable cost for the treadmills, completing the table below.**

| Output level of treadmills | Total variable cost £ |
|:---:|:---:|
| 1,000 | |
| 10,000 | |
| 25,000 | |
| 100,000 | |

## Task 3.8

The managing director of Munich Ltd wants to know the total production costs for the treadmills.

Use the table below to fill in the figures which you have already calculated and also work out the cost per unit at each level of production.

| Units | 1,000 £ | 10,000 £ | 25,000 £ | 100,000 £ |
|---|---|---|---|---|
| Costs | | | | |
| Variable | | | | |
| Fixed | | | | |
| Total production cost | ===== | ===== | ===== | ===== |
| Cost per unit | _____ | _____ | _____ | _____ |

## Task 3.9

Using the information in row 1 of the table below, complete the remaining rows with the fixed costs, variable costs, total costs and unit cost at the different levels of production.

| Units | Fixed costs £ | Variable costs £ | Total costs £ | Unit cost £ |
|---|---|---|---|---|
| 1,000 | 37,200 | 19,800 | 57,000 | 57.00 |
| 2,000 | | | | |
| 3,000 | | | | |
| 4,000 | | | | |

## Task 3.10

A business's single product has the following variable costs per unit.

Materials                                £4.50

Labour                                   £12.60

The business's total fixed costs are £75,000.

**Complete the following total cost and unit cost table for a production level of 15,000 units.**

| Element | Total cost £ | Unit cost £ |
|---|---|---|
| Materials | | |
| Labour | | |
| Overheads | | |
| Total | | |

## Task 3.11

A business makes a single product. At a production level of 27,500 units the business has the following cost details:

Materials              0.2 kilos are used per unit. Materials cost £25 per kilo.

Labour                 7,000 hours at £10.50 an hour

Fixed overheads   £35,000

**Complete the table below to show the total cost at the production level of 27,500 units.**

| Element | Cost £ |
|---|---|
| Materials | |
| Labour | |
| Overheads | |
| Total | |

# Chapter 4 Inventory classification and valuation

## Task 4.1

Patties Pastries is a bakery and cake shop.

**Classify the following items of inventory as raw materials, part-finished goods or finished goods. Tick the correct box.**

| Cost | Raw materials | Part-finished goods | Finished goods |
|---|---|---|---|
| Christmas cakes left to mature | | | |
| Yeast for breads | | | |
| Simnel cakes in the cake shop | | | |

## Task 4.2

Patties Pastries wants to calculate the value of its inventory and has been told there are three methods it could use. The table below describes the three methods.

**Put a tick against the correct method for each description.**

| Description | FIFO | LIFO | AVCO |
|---|---|---|---|
| Will give the highest inventory value if costs are rising | | | |
| Is the best method if inventories are combined, for instance cake mixes | | | |
| Uses the cost of the most recent inventories when costing issues | | | |

## Task 4.3

Patties Pastries has issued 100 cake boxes from its stores to the cake shop. Calculate the balance left under the LIFO method using the data below.

| DATE | RECEIPTS | | ISSUES | |
|------|----------|------|--------|------|
| | Units | Cost | Units | Cost |
| April 10 | 60 | £120 | | |
| April 11 | 45 | £135 | | |
| April 12 | 25 | £75 | | |
| April 19 | | | 100 | |
| April 27 | 70 | £210 | | |

**Complete the table below for the issue and closing inventory values.**

| Method | Cost of issue on 19 April £ | Closing inventory at 30 April £ |
|--------|------------------------------|----------------------------------|
| LIFO | | |

## Task 4.4

Patties Pastries buys in ingredients for its cake mix and issues these to the bakery where the cakes are made. In July it recorded the transactions below. Calculate the balance left under the AVCO method using the data below.

| DATE | RECEIPTS | | ISSUES | |
|------|----------|------|--------|------|
| | Tonnes | Cost | Tonnes | Cost |
| July 5 | 10 | £30 | | |
| July 11 | 15 | £45 | | |
| July 15 | 25 | £100 | | |
| July 19 | | | 40 | |
| July 28 | 30 | £150 | | |

**Complete the table below for the issue and closing inventory values.**

| Method | Cost of issue on 19 July £ | Closing inventory at 30 July £ |
|--------|-----------------------------|---------------------------------|
| AVCO | | |

## Task 4.5

Complete an inventory record card for the transactions in the Task 4.4 using the pro forma below.

| Inventory Record Card | | | | | | | | |
|---|---|---|---|---|---|---|---|---|
| | Purchases | | | Issues | | | Balance | |
| Date | Quantity | Cost per tonne | Total cost | Quantity | Cost per tonne | Total cost | Quantity | Total cost |
| | | £ | £ | £ | £ | £ | £ | £ |
| Balance at 1 July | | | | | | | | |
| 5 July | | | | | | | | |
| 11 July | | | | | | | | |
| 15 July | | | | | | | | |
| 19 July | | | | | | | | |
| 28 July | | | | | | | | |

## Task 4.6

A business has the following movements in a certain type of inventory into and out of its stores for the month of May:

| DATE | RECEIPTS | | ISSUES |
|---|---|---|---|
| | Units | Cost | Units |
| 5 May | 500 | £1,200 | |
| 9 May | 1,100 | £2,750 | |
| 13 May | | | 1,450 |
| 17 May | 400 | £1,100 | |
| 23 May | 250 | £700 | |

Complete the table below for the issue and closing inventory values.

| Method | Cost of Issue on 13 May £ | Closing Inventory at 31 May £ |
|---|---|---|
| FIFO | | |
| LIFO | | |
| AVCO | | |

## Task 4.7

Reorder the following headings and costs into a manufacturing account format on the right side of the table below for the year ended 31 December.

| Heading | £ | Heading | £ |
|---|---|---|---|
| Manufacturing overheads | 127,200 | | |
| Purchases of raw materials | 120,000 | | |
| COST OF GOODS MANUFACTURED | 570,700 | | |
| Closing inventory of raw materials | 24,000 | | |
| Direct Labour | 232,800 | | |
| COST OF GOODS SOLD | 582,700 | | |
| Closing inventory of work in progress | 24,000 | | |
| Direct expenses | 102,700 | | |
| MANUFACTURING COST | 575,500 | | |
| Opening inventory of work in progress | 19,200 | | |
| Opening inventory of raw materials | 16,800 | | |
| Opening inventory of finished goods | 72,000 | | |
| DIRECT MATERIALS USED | 112,800 | | |
| Closing inventory of finished goods | 60,000 | | |
| DIRECT COST | 448,300 | | |

# Chapter 5 Classifying labour costs

## Task 5.1

Luanne runs a beauty salon and employs three assistants. They normally work a 35-hour week with a basic wage of £8.50 per hour. If they work overtime they are paid this at time-and-a-half.

**Use the table below to complete the pay calculations for all three assistants for last week.**

| Assistant | Hours worked | Basic wage £ | Overtime £ | Gross wage £ |
|-----------|--------------|--------------|------------|--------------|
| Betty | 35 | | | |
| Hettie | 38 | | | |
| Lettie | 41 | | | |

## Task 5.2

Luanne has now decided to pay her assistants according only to the number of treatments they provide in a week.

The rate used is £15 per treatment successfully completed.

**Calculate the gross wage for the week for the assistants in the table below.**

| Assistant | Treatments successfully completed in a week | Gross wage £ |
|-----------|---------------------------------------------|--------------|
| Betty | 16 | |
| Hettie | 20 | |
| Lettie | 23 | |

## Task 5.3

Luanne has decided to pay Lettie a bonus for her hard work.

**Using the information in the previous task, calculate how much Lettie would earn if Luanne paid her an extra £1.50 per treatment for the treatments she completed where these exceed 20 in a week. Enter your answer in the table.**

| Assistant | Treatments done | Gross wage £ | Bonus £ | Gross wage + bonus £ |
|---|---|---|---|---|
| Lettie | 23 | | | |

## Task 5.4

Luanne has been on a seminar where the speaker referred to the benefits of using piecework and time-rate payments. Luanne unfortunately forgot to take full notes and has asked you to fill in the gaps in her notes, which are in the form of a table.

**Refer to the table and tick the correct column.**

| Payment method | Time- rate | Piecework |
|---|---|---|
| Quality is a priority as pay is the same no matter how much is produced | | |
| This method gives employees an incentive to produce more | | |

## Task 5.5

Luanne is wondering whether to adopt a signing-in system for her three hairdressers. At the seminar the speaker outlined the features of three types of signing-in system. Luanne is a bit confused as she cannot remember which description refers to which system.

**You can help her out by ticking the correct box in her notes.**

| Description | Attendance record | Signing-in book | Clock cards |
|---|---|---|---|
| Each assistant has a swipe card, which is used to register the time of commencing and finishing work | | | |
| A page for each assistant who signs when entering or leaving the building | | | |
| A calendar for each assistant that records their presence at work by a tick in a box | | | |

## Task 5.6

Luanne has adopted a clock card system for her three hairdressers. They are still paid at £8.50 per hour for a 35-hour week. Overtime is now paid at time-and-a-half for time worked in excess of seven hours on each weekday, and double time for any work done on a day at the weekend.

| | Hours worked | | |
|---|---|---|---|
| | Betty | Lettie | Hettie |
| Monday | 7 | 8 | 7.25 |
| Tuesday | 7 | 8 | 7 |
| Wednesday | 8.5 | 7.5 | 7 |
| Thursday | 7 | 8 | 7 |
| Friday | 7 | 7.5 | 7 |
| Saturday | 3 | | 2 |

**Calculate the gross pay of the hairdressers based on the clock card information above and enter the details in the table below.**

| | Betty £ | Lettie £ | Hettie £ |
|---|---|---|---|
| Total hours | | | |
| Basic pay | | | |
| Pay at time-and-a-half | | | |
| Pay at double time | | | |
| Total gross pay | | | |

## Task 5.7

A business pays a time-rate of £12 per hour to its direct labour for a standard 40-hour week. Any of the labour force working in excess of 40 hours is paid an overtime rate of time and a third per hour

**Calculate the gross wage for the week for the two workers in the table below.**

| Worker | Hours Worked | Basic wage £ | Overtime £ | Gross wage £ |
|---|---|---|---|---|
| B Calnan | 40 hours | | | |
| N Imai | 43 hours | | | |

## Task 5.8

A business uses a piecework method to pay labour in one of its workshops. The rate used is £2.30 per unit produced.

**Calculate the gross wage for the week for the two workers in the table below.**

| Worker | Units produced in week | Gross wage £ |
|---|---|---|
| L Akinola | 187 units | |
| J Dunwoody | 203 units | |

# Chapter 6 Coding costs

## Task 6.1

Alexis runs a successful boat building business within Europe, which exports boats to Asia. His accountant recently recommended a coding system to help Alexis classify his costs and revenues. Each cost or revenue is classified in accordance with the table below. Thus a boat sale to Japan would be 9/200.

**Use the table to code the transactions listed below.**

| Cost | Code 1 | | Code 2 |
|---|---|---|---|
| Sales | 9 | European sales | 100 |
| | | Asian sales | 200 |
| Production | 8 | Direct cost | 100 |
| | | Indirect cost | 200 |
| Administration | 7 | Direct cost | 100 |
| | | Indirect cost | 200 |
| Selling and Distribution | 6 | Direct cost | 100 |
| | | Indirect cost | 200 |

**Code the following revenue and cost transactions for Alexis, which have been extracted from purchase invoices, sales invoices and payroll, using the table below.**

| Transaction | Code |
|---|---|
| Electricity charge for the upstairs offices | |
| Mobile call charges for sales reps | |
| Sales to Malaysia | |
| Sales to Italy | |
| Brass handles for boat decks | |
| Factory supervisor wages | |

## Task 6.2

Alexis would also like to analyse his costs according to whether they are materials, labour or overheads. He is looking at a coding system that classifies costs by their elements of cost (materials, labour or overheads) and then further classifies each element by nature (direct or indirect cost) where relevant as below. So, for example, the code for direct materials is M100.

| Element of Cost | Code | Nature of Cost | Code |
|---|---|---|---|
| Materials | M | Direct | 100 |
|  |  | Indirect | 200 |
| Labour | L | Direct | 100 |
|  |  | Indirect | 200 |
| Overheads | O | Direct | 100 |
|  |  | Indirect | 200 |

**Code the following costs, extracted from invoices and payroll, using the table below.**

| Cost | Code |
|---|---|
| Wages of boat builders |  |
| Fees for bookkeeper |  |
| Cost of buying timber |  |
| Lubricants for lathes |  |
| Business rates on Alexis' showroom |  |

## Task 6.3

Alexis has now adopted a coding system and has been using it for some months now. He has asked you to update the code balances for July using the data below.

| Code | Costs incurred in July £ |
|---|---|
| 010101 | 125.00 |
| 010102 | 3,000.40 |
| 010103 | 1,125.80 |
| 010202 | 433.20 |
| 010203 | 1,210.54 |
| 010301 | 44.00 |
| 010303 | 1,450.00 |

**You will need to enter the costs incurred into the table below, which has the opening balances for July, and work out the closing balances at 31 July.**

| Code | Opening balance £ | Update £ | Closing balance 31 July £ |
|---|---|---|---|
| 010101 | 7,456.98 | | |
| 010102 | 6,779.20 | | |
| 010103 | 3,556.90 | | |
| 010201 | 667.23 | | |
| 010202 | 674.55 | | |
| 010203 | 5,634.01 | | |
| 010301 | 356.35 | | |
| 010302 | 362.00 | | |
| 010303 | 12,563.98 | | |

## Task 6.4

A manufacturer of porcelain and earthenware coffee cups uses a numerical coding structure based on one profit centre and three cost centres as outlined below. Each code has a sub-code so each transaction will be coded as **/**.

| Profit/Cost Centre [Picklist] | Code | Sub-classification [Picklist] | Sub-code |
|---|---|---|---|
| Sales | 01 | Porcelain Sales | 01 |
| | | Earthenware Sales | 02 |
| Production | 02 | Direct Cost | 01 |
| | | Indirect Cost | 02 |
| Selling and Distribution | 03 | Direct Cost | 01 |
| | | Indirect Cost | 02 |
| Administration | 04 | Direct Cost | 01 |
| | | Indirect Cost | 02 |

**The codes have been used for a number of items in November. Identify from each code the profit or cost centre and the sub-classification to which it relates.**

| Code | Profit/Cost Centre | Sub-classification |
|---|---|---|
| 04/02 | ▼ | ▼ |
| 02/02 | ▼ | ▼ |
| 03/02 | ▼ | ▼ |
| 01/02 | ▼ | ▼ |
| 02/01 | ▼ | ▼ |
| 04/02 | ▼ | ▼ |
| 01/01 | ▼ | ▼ |

**Picklist:**

Administration
Selling and Distribution
Sales
Production
Direct Cost
Indirect Cost
Earthenware Sales
Porcelain Sales

# Chapter 7 Comparison of costs and income

## Task 7.1

Siegfried Ltd has recently introduced a variance analysis reporting system. The managing director would like you to calculate the variances for the figures in the table, and let him know whether these are favourable or adverse.

**Calculate the amount of the variance for each cost type and then determine whether it is adverse or favourable by typing F for favourable and A for adverse in the right-hand column of the table below.**

| Cost type | Budget £ | Actual £ | Variance £ | Adverse/ Favourable |
|---|---|---|---|---|
| Direct materials | 24,390 | 25,430 | | |
| Direct labour | 11,270 | 12,380 | | |
| Production overheads | 5,340 | 5,160 | | |
| Administration overheads | 4,990 | 4,770 | | |
| Selling and Distribution overheads | 2,040 | 2,460 | | |

## Task 7.2

It is now one month later and the managing director has asked you to analyse the variances summarised in the table below. You need to indicate whether they are significant or not significant using the dropdown boxes.

In Siegfried Ltd, any variance in excess of 5% of budget is deemed to be significant and should be reported to the relevant manager for review and appropriate action.

**Examine the variances in the table below and select the correct option for the right-hand column.**

| Cost type | Budget £ | Variance £ | Adverse/ Favourable | Significant/ Not significant |
|---|---|---|---|---|
| Direct materials | 23,780 | 360 | Adverse | ▼ |
| Direct labour | 10,460 | 660 | Favourable | ▼ |
| Production overheads | 5,330 | 318 | Adverse | ▼ |
| Administration overheads | 4,220 | 70 | Favourable | ▼ |
| Selling and Distribution overheads | 1,990 | 10 | Adverse | ▼ |

**Picklist:**

Significant

Not significant

## Task 7.3

The managing director of Siegfried Ltd wants to know more about how budgets work. He has sent you a memo and asked you to confirm whether the statements he has made are correct.

**Show if the following statements are True or False by putting a tick in the relevant column of the table below.**

| Statement | True ✓ | False ✓ |
|---|---|---|
| An adverse variance means actual costs are greater than budgeted costs | | |
| A favourable variance means budgeted costs are greater than actual costs | | |

## Task 7.4

A business has reported actual costs and variances as set out in the table below.

**In each case, identify what the budgeted cost would have been.**

| Cost | Actual cost £ | Variance £ | Budgeted cost £ |
|---|---|---|---|
| Production overheads | 12,256 | 52 F | |
| Sales and distribution labour | 8,407 | 109 A | |
| Administration consumables | 4,751 | 236 A | |

## Task 7.5

The following data is available about Campbell Ltd's costs and income:

- October: Variable costs £55,000, Fixed costs £22,000, Income £140,000
- November: Variable costs £39,000, Fixed costs £22,000, Income £135,000
- December: Variable costs £50,000, Fixed costs £30,000, Income £150,000

You have been asked to prepare a report for Campbell Ltd's management showing:

(a) Its total costs in each month and for the quarter
(b) Its profit or loss for each month and for the quarter

**Prepare the following spreadsheet to calculate and present this data clearly:**

| | A | B Variable costs £ | C Fixed costs £ | D Total costs £ | E Income £ | F Profit/(loss) £ |
|---|---|---|---|---|---|---|
| 2 | October | | | | | |
| 3 | November | | | | | |
| 4 | December | | | | | |
| 5 | Quarter | | | | | |

## Task 7.6

Insert the formula that you would use for each of the following cells from the spreadsheet in Task 7.5:

| Cell reference | Formula |
|---|---|
| Cell D2 | |
| Cell F3 | |
| Cell E5 | |

..................................................................................

## Task 7.7

A spreadsheet has been prepared for Campbell Ltd. It compares budgeted income and costs for January with actual income and costs. The managers wish to know which variances are significant. They regard a variance as significant if it is more than 5% different from budget.

(a) **Insert figures for variances, and indicate whether each one is adverse or favourable by using picklist 1.**

(b) **Calculate each variance as a percentage of the budgeted figure, correct to one decimal place.**

(c) **Indicate whether each variance is significant or not significant by using picklist 2.**

| | A | B | C | D | E | F | G |
|---|---|---|---|---|---|---|---|
| | | Budget £ | Actual £ | Variance £ | Adverse/ Favourable | Variance as percentage of budget % | Significant/ Not significant |
| 2 | Sales | 170,000 | 162,000 | | ▼ | | ▼ |
| 3 | Variable costs | 68,000 | 62,000 | | ▼ | | ▼ |
| 4 | Fixed costs | 25,000 | 30,000 | | ▼ | | ▼ |
| 5 | Profit | 77,000 | 70,000 | | ▼ | | ▼ |

**Picklist 1**

Adverse
Favourable

**Picklist 2**

Significant
Not significant

································································································

## Task 7.8

**Insert the formula that you would use for each of the following cells from the spreadsheet in Task 7.7:**

| Cell reference | Formula |
|---|---|
| Cell D3 | |
| Cell F4 | |

································································································

# Answer bank

**Answer bank**

# Basic Costing Answer bank

## Chapter 1

### Task 1.1

| Definition | Cash transaction | Credit transaction |
|---|---|---|
| Transactions whereby payment is immediate | ✓ | |
| Transactions whereby payment is to be made at some future date | | ✓ |

### Task 1.2

| Definition | Assets | Liabilities |
|---|---|---|
| Amounts that the business owes | | ✓ |
| Amounts that the business owns | ✓ | |

### Task 1.3

| Definition | Management accounting system | Financial accounting system |
|---|---|---|
| Recording transactions of the organisation in the ledgers to prepare financial statements | | ✓ |
| Recording transactions of the organisation to provide useful information for management | ✓ | |

## Task 1.4

| Definition | Budgets | Cost centre | Variances |
|---|---|---|---|
| An area of the organisation for which costs are collected together for management accounting purposes | | ✓ | |
| Differences that arise when the actual results of the organisation differ from the budgeted results | | | ✓ |
| Plans of the organisation for the next year in terms of money and/or resources | ✓ | | |

## Task 1.5

| Activity | Planning | Decision-making | Control |
|---|---|---|---|
| Whether to expand the business | | ✓ | |
| Budgeting how many products to produce | ✓ | | |
| Regular comparison of actual activities to plans and budgets | | | ✓ |
| Reporting variances | | | ✓ |
| Management preparing strategic and operational plans | ✓ | | |
| Management deciding which suppliers to use | | ✓ | |

## Task 1.6

| Description | Sole trader | Partnership | Limited company |
|---|---|---|---|
| A group of individuals who trade together to make a profit | | ✓ | |
| A business where the owner trades in their own name | ✓ | | |
| The owners delegate the running of the business to managers | | | ✓ |

BPP
LEARNING MEDIA

## Task 1.7

| Transaction | Capital | Revenue |
|---|---|---|
| Purchase of a motor car for the managing director in a printing business | ✓ | |
| Purchase of a motor car by a garage for resale | | ✓ |
| Payment of wages | | ✓ |
| Rent on a workshop | | ✓ |
| Extension works on a workshop | ✓ | |
| Office furniture for the managing director | ✓ | |

## Task 1.8

| Description | Manufacturing | Retail | Service |
|---|---|---|---|
| Accountants, lawyers and other businesses which don't manufacture or sell a physical product | | | ✓ |
| The business buys in raw materials for making goods | ✓ | | |
| The business buys in ready-made goods which it sells on | | ✓ | |

## Task 1.9

| Definition | ✓ |
|---|---|
| To make decisions based on the best available data | |
| To control resources | |
| To record and accurately classify the transactions of the business | ✓ |
| To find the money to fund the owner's lifestyle | |

## Task 1.10

| Characteristic | Financial accounting system | Management accounting system |
|---|---|---|
| It supports managers in their control activities | | ✓ |
| In a company it enables the production of accounts in a format required by law | ✓ | |
| It provides information to assist in management decision making | | ✓ |
| It ensures that all transactions are correctly classified as relating to assets, liabilities, capital, income or expenses | ✓ | |

## Chapter 2

### Task 2.1

| Cost | Materials | Labour | Overheads |
|---|:---:|:---:|:---:|
| Glaze for the mosaic tiles | ✓ | | |
| Gas charges for heating the workshop | | | ✓ |
| Employees mixing the glazes for the tiles | | ✓ | |
| Clay used in making the tiles | ✓ | | |

### Task 2.2

| Cost | Direct | Indirect |
|---|:---:|:---:|
| Wine bought in from a wholesaler | ✓ | |
| Business rates for the bistro | | ✓ |
| Wages of waiters and waitresses | ✓ | |
| Salary of shop manager | | ✓ |

### Task 2.3

| Cost | Production | Administration | Selling and Distribution | Finance |
|---|:---:|:---:|:---:|:---:|
| Purchase of strings for making guitars | ✓ | | | |
| Advertising the instruments in the city tourist information shop | | | ✓ | |
| Wages of the bookkeeper | | ✓ | | |
| Salaries of craftsmen making the instruments | ✓ | | | |
| Interest charged on business overdraft | | | | ✓ |

BPP
LEARNING MEDIA

## Task 2.4

| Cost | Material | Labour | Overheads |
|---|---|---|---|
| Wages of pastry cooks | | ✓ | |
| Salesperson's salary for the year | | | ✓ |
| Confectioner's cream used to fill the pies | ✓ | | |
| Gas charges for the ovens | | | ✓ |

## Task 2.5

| Description | Basic pay | Overtime | Bonus |
|---|---|---|---|
| Amount paid for ordinary hours of work | ✓ | | |
| Hours worked above the normal hours stated in the employment contract | | ✓ | |
| Additional income for working more efficiently | | | ✓ |

## Task 2.6

| Description of cost | Direct materials | Direct labour | Indirect materials | Indirect labour | Indirect expenses |
|---|---|---|---|---|---|
| Factory supervisor's wages | | | | ✓ | |
| Lubricant for machinery | | | ✓ | | |
| Leather used to make shoes | ✓ | | | | |
| Hairdresser in a hair salon | | ✓ | | | |
| Telephone rental for administration office | | | | | ✓ |

## Task 2.7

| Expense | Specific | Joint |
|---|:---:|:---:|
| Repair of machinery used by one production line only | ✓ | |
| Rent of workshop housing three cost centres | | ✓ |
| Business rates for the workshop housing three cost centres | | ✓ |
| Stationery used by the administration and payroll departments | | ✓ |
| Photocopier used by the managing director's personal assistant only | ✓ | |

## Task 2.8

| Transaction | Capital | Revenue |
|---|:---:|:---:|
| Installation of new machinery | ✓ | |
| Breakdown repairs on a faulty machine | | ✓ |
| Fees of bookkeeper | | ✓ |
| Purchase of new car for salesperson | ✓ | |

# Task 2.9

| Cost centre expense | Working | £ |
|---|---|---|
| Grinding – rent | £4,500 × 30% | 1,350 |
| Grinding – overhaul | | 750 |
| Total Grinding | | 2,100 |
| Assembly – rent | £4,500 × 25% | 1,125 |
| Assembly – safety testing | | 400 |
| Total Assembly | | 1,525 |
| Testing – rent | £4,500 × 15% | 675 |
| Despatch – rent | £2,500 × 30% | 750 |
| Stores – rent | £2,500 × 70% | 1,750 |
| Security – rent | £4,500 × 10% | 450 |
| Sales – rent | £1,000 × 50% | 500 |
| Sales – training | | 500 |
| Total Sales | | 1,000 |
| Canteen – rent | £4,500 × 20% | 900 |
| Administration – rent | £1,000 × 50% | 500 |

# Task 2.10

| Cost | Materials | Labour | Overheads |
|---|---|---|---|
| Telephone costs for call centre | | | ✓ |
| Rent on call centre building | | | ✓ |
| Printer paper used for certificates of insurance sent to clients | ✓ | | |
| Salaries of client advisers | | ✓ | |

## Task 2.11

| Cost | Direct | Indirect |
|---|---|---|
| Rent of booking office | | ✓ |
| Diesel for taxis | ✓ | |
| Wages of taxi drivers | ✓ | |
| Licence for firm from taxi regulator | | ✓ |

## Test 2.12

| Cost | Production | Administration | Selling and Distribution |
|---|---|---|---|
| Wages of workers making sandwiches | ✓ | | |
| Fee for website maintenance | | ✓ | |
| Purchases of bread | ✓ | | |
| Fuel for delivery vehicle | | | ✓ |

# Chapter 3

## Task 3.1

| Cost | Variable | Semi-variable | Fixed |
|------|----------|---------------|-------|
| Employee paid a basic wage plus commission based on production quantity | | ✓ | |
| Rent of the factory workshop | | | ✓ |
| Print ink used for letterheads and logos | ✓ | | |

## Task 3.2

| Cost | Production cost centre | Service cost centre | Profit centre |
|------|------------------------|---------------------|---------------|
| Selling and marketing the products in the retail shop | | | ✓ |
| Mixing, filling and packing the sausages | ✓ | | |
| Storage in freezers in the warehouse | | ✓ | |

## Task 3.3

| Cost | Audit | Tax | Personnel |
|------|-------|-----|-----------|
| Payroll software for paying salaries and wages | | | ✓ |
| Annual purchase of software updated for the year's Finance Act for the tax advisors | | ✓ | |
| Subscription to an audit advice helpline | ✓ | | |

## Task 3.4

| Cost | True | False |
|---|---|---|
| Many fixed costs are only fixed over a certain range of output | ✓ | |
| Variable cost per unit falls as output rises | | ✓ |
| Direct costs are generally variable | ✓ | |
| Fixed cost per unit rises as output rises | | ✓ |

## Task 3.5

| Cost | True | False |
|---|---|---|
| In a service organisation the Human Resources department is likely to be classified as a cost centre | ✓ | |
| Distribution would not be a cost centre in a manufacturing organisation | | ✓ |
| Stores could be a cost centre in a manufacturing or a service organisation | ✓ | |

## Task 3.6

| Output level of treadmills | Fixed cost per treadmill £ |
|---|---|
| 1,000 | 50 |
| 10,000 | 5 |
| 25,000 | 2 |
| 100,000 | 0.50 |

## Task 3.7

| Number of treadmills | Total variable cost £ |
|---|---|
| 1,000 | 35,000 |
| 10,000 | 350,000 |
| 25,000 | 875,000 |
| 100,000 | 3,500,000 |

## Task 3.8

| Units | 1,000 | 10,000 | 25,000 | 100,000 |
|---|---|---|---|---|
| | £ | £ | £ | £ |
| **Costs** | | | | |
| Variable (units × (£35)) | 35,000 | 350,000 | 875,000 | 3,500,000 |
| Fixed | 50,000 | 50,000 | 50,000 | 50,000 |
| **Total production cost** | 85,000 | 400,000 | 925,000 | 3,550,000 |
| Cost per unit | £85.00 | £40.00 | £37.00 | £35.50 |

## Task 3.9

| Units | Fixed costs £ | Variable costs £ | Total costs £ | Unit cost £ |
|---|---|---|---|---|
| 1,000 | 37,200 | 19,800 | 57,000 | 57.00 |
| 2,000 | 37,200 | 39,600 | 76,800 | 38.40 |
| 3,000 | 37,200 | 59,400 | 96,600 | 32.20 |
| 4,000 | 37,200 | 79,200 | 116,400 | 29.10 |

## Task 3.10

| Element | Total cost £ | Unit cost £ |
|---|---|---|
| Materials | 67,500 | 4.50 |
| Labour | 189,000 | 12.60 |
| Overheads | 75,000 | 5.00 |
| Total | 331,500 | 22.10 |

## Task 3.11

| Element | Cost £ |
|---|---|
| Materials | 137,500 |
| Labour | 73,500 |
| Overheads | 35,000 |
| Total | 246,000 |

# Chapter 4

## Task 4.1

| Cost | Raw materials | Part-finished goods | Finished goods |
|---|---|---|---|
| Christmas cakes left to mature | | ✓ | |
| Yeast for breads | ✓ | | |
| Simnel cakes in the cake shop | | | ✓ |

## Task 4.2

| Description | FIFO | LIFO | AVCO |
|---|---|---|---|
| Will give the highest inventory value if costs are rising | ✓ | | |
| Is the best method if inventories are combined, for instance cake mixes | | | ✓ |
| Uses the cost of the most recent inventories when costing issues | | ✓ | |

## Task 4.3

The cost of the issue on 19 April under LIFO is £75 + £135 + (30 x £120/60) = £270.

Closing inventory at 30 April consists of 30 units at £120/60 = £60, plus the receipt of 70 units for £210.

| Method | Cost of issue on 19 April £ | Closing inventory at 30 April £ |
|---|---|---|
| LIFO | 270 | 270 |

## Task 4.4

| Method | Cost of issue on 19 July £ | Closing inventory at 30 July £ |
|---|---|---|
| AVCO | 140 | 185 |

## Task 4.5

| | Inventory Record Card | | | | | | | |
|---|---|---|---|---|---|---|---|---|
| | Purchases | | | Issues | | | Balance | |
| Date | Quantity | Cost per tonne | Total cost | Quantity | Cost per tonne | Total cost | Quantity | Total cost |
| | | £ | £ | £ | £ | £ | £ | £ |
| Balance at 1 July | | | | | | | 0 | 0 |
| 5 July | 10 | 3.00 | 30 | | | | 10 | 30 |
| 11 July | 15 | 3.00 | 45 | | | | 25 | 75 |
| 15 July | 25 | 4.00 | 100 | | | | 50 | 175 |
| 19 July | | | | 40 | 3.50 | 140 | 10 | 35 |
| 28 July | 30 | 5.00 | 150 | | | | 40 | 185 |

## Task 4.6

| Method | Cost of issue on 13 May £ | Closing inventory at 31 May £ |
|---|---|---|
| FIFO | 1,200 + (950 × 2,750/1,100) = **3,575** | 700 + 1,100 + (150 × 2,750/1,100) = **2,175** |
| LIFO | 2,750 + (350 × 1,200/500) = **3,590** | 700 + 1,100 + (150 × 1,200/500) = **2,160** |
| AVCO | 1,450/1,600 × (1,200 + 2,750) = **3,580** | 700 + 1,100 + (150/1,600 × (1,200 + 2,750)) = **2,170** |

# Task 4.7

| Heading | £ | Heading | £ |
|---|---|---|---|
| Manufacturing overheads | 127,200 | Opening Inventory of Raw Materials | 16,800 |
| Purchases of raw materials | 120,000 | Purchases of Raw Materials | 120,000 |
| COST OF GOODS MANUFACTURED | 570,700 | Closing Inventory of Raw Materials | (24,000) |
| Closing inventory of raw materials | 24,000 | DIRECT MATERIALS USED | 112,800 |
| Direct Labour | 232,800 | Direct Labour | 232,800 |
| COST OF GOODS SOLD | 582,700 | Direct Expenses | 102,700 |
| Closing inventory of work in progress | 24,000 | DIRECT COST | 448,300 |
| Direct expenses | 102,700 | Manufacturing Overheads | 127,200 |
| MANUFACTURING COST | 575,500 | MANUFACTURING COST | 575,500 |
| Opening inventory of work in progress | 19,200 | Opening Inventory of Work in Progress | 19,200 |
| Opening inventory of raw materials | 16,800 | Closing Inventory of Work in Progress | (24,000) |
| Opening inventory of finished goods | 72,000 | COST OF GOODS MANUFACTURED | 570,700 |
| DIRECT MATERIALS USED | 112,800 | Opening Inventory of Finished Goods | 72,000 |
| Closing inventory of finished goods | 60,000 | Closing Inventory of Finished Goods | (60,000) |
| DIRECT COST | 448,300 | COST OF GOODS SOLD | 582,700 |

# Chapter 5

## Task 5.1

| Assistant | Hours worked | Basic wage £ | Overtime £ | Gross wage £ |
|---|---|---|---|---|
| Betty | 35 | 297.50 | 0 | 297.50 |
| Hettie | 38 | 297.50 | 38.25 | 335.75 |
| Lettie | 41 | 297.50 | 76.50 | 374.00 |

## Task 5.2

| Assistant | Treatments successfully completed in a week | Gross wage £ |
|---|---|---|
| Betty | 16 | 240 |
| Hettie | 20 | 300 |
| Lettie | 23 | 345 |

## Task 5.3

| Assistant | Treatments done | Gross wage £ | Bonus £ | Gross wage + bonus £ |
|---|---|---|---|---|
| Lettie | 23 | 345 | 4.50 | 349.50 |

## Task 5.4

| Payment method | Time- rate | Piecework |
|---|---|---|
| Quality is a priority as pay is the same no matter how much is produced | ✓ | |
| This method gives employees an incentive to produce more | | ✓ |

## Task 5.5

| Description | Attendance record | Signing-in book | Clock cards |
|---|---|---|---|
| Each assistant has a swipe card, which is used to register the time of commencing and finishing work | | | ✓ |
| A page for each assistant who signs when entering or leaving the building | | ✓ | |
| A calendar for each assistant that records their presence at work by a tick in a box | ✓ | | |

## Task 5.6

| | Betty £ | Lettie £ | Hettie £ |
|---|---|---|---|
| Total hours | 39.50 | 39.00 | 37.25 |
| Basic pay (35 × £8.50) | 297.50 | 297.50 | 297.50 |
| Pay at time-and-a-half | 1.5 × 8.50 × 1.5 = **19.12** | 4 × 8.50 × 1.5 = **51.00** | 0.25 × 8.50 × 1.5 = **3.19** |
| Pay at double time | 3 × 8.50 × 2 = **51.00** | 0 | 2 × 8.50 × 2 = **34.00** |
| Total gross pay | 367.62 | 348.50 | 334.69 |

## Task 5.7

| Worker | Hours worked | Basic wage £ | Overtime £ | Gross wage £ |
|---|---|---|---|---|
| B Calnan | 40 hours | 480.00 | 0 | 480.00 |
| N Imai | 43 hours | 480.00 | 48.00 | 528.00 |

## Task 5.8

| Worker | Units produced in week | Gross wage £ |
|---|---|---|
| L Akinola | 187 units | 430.10 |
| J Dunwoody | 203 units | 466.90 |

# Chapter 6

## Task 6.1

| Transaction | Code |
|---|---|
| Electricity charge for the upstairs offices | 7/200 |
| Mobile call charges for sales reps | 6/200 |
| Sales to Malaysia | 9/200 |
| Sales to Italy | 9/100 |
| Brass handles for boat decks | 8/100 |
| Factory supervisor wages | 8/200 |

## Task 6.2

| Cost | Code |
|---|---|
| Wages of boat builders | L100 |
| Fees for bookkeeper | O200 |
| Cost of buying timber | M100 |
| Lubricants for lathes | M200 |
| Business rates on Alexis' showroom | O200 |

## Task 6.3

| Code | Opening balance | Update | Closing balance 31 July |
|---|---|---|---|
| | £ | £ | £ |
| 010101 | 7,456.98 | 125.00 | 7,581.98 |
| 010102 | 6,779.20 | 3,000.40 | 9,779.60 |
| 010103 | 3,556.90 | 1,125.80 | 4,682.70 |
| 010201 | 667.23 | 0 | 667.23 |
| 010202 | 674.55 | 433.20 | 1,107.75 |
| 010203 | 5,634.01 | 1,210.54 | 6,844.55 |
| 010301 | 356.35 | 44.00 | 400.35 |
| 010302 | 362.00 | 0 | 362.00 |
| 010303 | 12,563.98 | 1,450.00 | 14,013.98 |

## Task 6.4

| Code | Profit/Cost Centre | Sub-classification |
|---|---|---|
| 04/02 | Administration | Indirect cost |
| 02/02 | Production | Indirect cost |
| 03/02 | Selling and Distribution | Indirect cost |
| 01/02 | Sales | Earthenware sales |
| 02/01 | Production | Direct cost |
| 04/02 | Administration | Indirect cost |
| 01/01 | Sales | Porcelain sales |

# Chapter 7

## Task 7.1

| Cost type | Budget £ | Actual £ | Variance £ | Adverse/Favourable |
|---|---|---|---|---|
| Direct materials | 24,390 | 25,430 | 1,040 | A |
| Direct labour | 11,270 | 12,380 | 1,110 | A |
| Production overheads | 5,340 | 5,160 | 180 | F |
| Administration overheads | 4,990 | 4,770 | 220 | F |
| Selling and Distribution overheads | 2,040 | 2,460 | 420 | A |

## Task 7.2

| Cost type | Budget £ | Variance £ | Adverse/ Favourable | Significant/ Not significant |
|---|---|---|---|---|
| Direct materials | 23,780 | 360 | Adverse | Not significant |
| Direct labour | 10,460 | 660 | Favourable | Significant |
| Production overheads | 5,330 | 318 | Adverse | Significant |
| Administration overheads | 4,220 | 70 | Favourable | Not significant |
| Selling and Distribution overheads | 1,990 | 10 | Adverse | Not significant |

## Task 7.3

| Statement | True | False |
|---|---|---|
| An adverse variance means actual costs are greater than budgeted costs | ✓ | |
| A favourable variance means budgeted costs are greater than actual costs | ✓ | |

## Task 7.4

| Cost | Actual cost £ | Variance £ | Budgeted cost £ |
|---|---|---|---|
| Production overheads | 12,256 | 52 F | 12,308 |
| Sales and distribution labour | 8,407 | 109 A | 8,298 |
| Administration consumables | 4,751 | 236 A | 4,515 |

## Task 7.5

| | A | B Variable costs £ | C Fixed costs £ | D Total costs £ | E Income £ | F Profit/(loss £ |
|---|---|---|---|---|---|---|
| 2 | October | 55,000 | 22,000 | 77,000 | 140,000 | 63,000 |
| 3 | November | 39,000 | 22,000 | 61,000 | 135,000 | 74,000 |
| 4 | December | 50,000 | 30,000 | 80,000 | 150,000 | 70,000 |
| 5 | Quarter | 144,000 | 74,000 | 218,000 | 425,000 | 207,000 |

## Task 7.6

| Cell reference | Formula |
|---|---|
| Cell D2 | = (B2+C2) |
| Cell F3 | = (E3–D3) |
| Cell E5 | = SUM(E2:E4) OR = (E2+E3+E4) |

## Task 7.7

| | A | B | C | D | E | F | G |
|---|---|---|---|---|---|---|---|
| | | Budget £ | Actual £ | Variance £ | Adverse/ Favourable | Variance as percentage of budget % | Significant/ Not significant |
| 2 | Sales | 170,000 | 162,000 | 8,000 | Adverse | 4.7 | Not significant |
| 3 | Variable costs | 68,000 | 62,000 | 6,000 | Favourable | 8.8 | Significant |
| 4 | Fixed costs | 25,000 | 30,000 | 5,000 | Adverse | 20.0 | Significant |
| 5 | Profit | 77,000 | 70,000 | 7,000 | Adverse | 9.1 | Significant |

## Task 7.8

| Cell reference | Formula |
|---|---|
| Cell D3 | = (B3–C3) |
| Cell F4 | = (D4/B4) |

**Answer bank**

# AAT AQ2013 SAMPLE ASSESSMENT
# BASIC COSTING

**Time allowed: 2 hours**

AAT AQ2013
SAMPLE ASSESSMENT

## Task 1 (8 marks)

Costing uses a number of techniques to assist management.

(a) **Identify the following statements as being true or false by putting a tick in the relevant column of the table below.**

| Statement | True | False |
|---|---|---|
| FIFO is a technique used to cost issues and to value inventories | ☐ | ☐ |
| The piecework method to pay labour guarantees a set amount of wages | ☐ | ☐ |
| A variance calculation measures the difference between revenue and cost | ☐ | ☐ |
| Classification of cost by behaviour allows the planning of total cost at differing levels of output | ☐ | ☐ |

The table below lists some of the characteristics of financial accounting and management accounting.

(b) **Indicate the characteristics for each system by putting a tick in the relevant column of the table below.**

| Characteristic | Financial Accounting | Management Accounting |
|---|---|---|
| This system produces statements that are used as a basis to determine the tax charge | ☐ | ☐ |
| This system uses techniques to cost issues and to value inventories | ☐ | ☐ |
| This system produces statements that are primarily for internal use | ☐ | ☐ |
| This system produces statements that have many external users | ☐ | ☐ |

## Task 2 (8 marks)

Nordeste Ltd is in business as a manufacturer of stationery.

(a) **Classify the following costs it incurred by element (material, labour or overhead) by putting a tick in the relevant column of the table below.**

| Cost | Material | Labour | Overhead |
|------|----------|--------|----------|
| Insurance of office computers | ☐ | ☐ | ☐ |
| Ink cartridges used in the production of pens | ☐ | ☐ | ☐ |
| Wages of employees in the production department | ☐ | ☐ | ☐ |
| Card used to produce binders for notebooks | ☐ | ☐ | ☐ |

Nordeste Ltd is in business as a manufacturer of stationery.

(b) **Classify the following costs incurred by nature (direct or indirect) by putting a tick in the relevant column of the table below.**

| Cost | Direct | Indirect |
|------|--------|----------|
| Insurance of factory | ☐ | ☐ |
| Paper used in the manufacture of envelopes | ☐ | ☐ |
| Salary of production manager | ☐ | ☐ |
| Plastic used in the production of pens | ☐ | ☐ |

## Task 3 (8 marks)

Squench Ltd produces fruit drinks.

(a) **Classify the following costs incurred by function (production, administration, selling and distribution or finance) by putting a tick in the relevant column of the table below.**

| Cost | Production | Administration | Selling and distribution | Finance |
|------|------------|----------------|--------------------------|---------|
| Fruit purchased for use in drinks | ☐ | ☐ | ☐ | ☐ |
| Stationery provided to all departments | ☐ | ☐ | ☐ | ☐ |
| Interest charged on bank loan | ☐ | ☐ | ☐ | ☐ |
| Sales campaign | ☐ | ☐ | ☐ | ☐ |

Squench Ltd produces fruit drinks.

(b) **Classify the following costs by their behaviour (fixed, variable or semi-variable) by putting a tick in the relevant column of the table below.**

| Cost | Fixed | Variable | Semi-variable |
|------|-------|----------|---------------|
| Employees in the bottling department paid on a piecework basis | ☐ | ☐ | ☐ |
| Annual consultancy charge for updating the website | ☐ | ☐ | ☐ |
| Sugar used in drinks | ☐ | ☐ | ☐ |
| Machinery hire consisting of a fixed rental charge and a usage charge | ☐ | ☐ | ☐ |

## Task 4 (6 marks)

Workout Ltd produces and sells sports and leisurewear. It uses a numerical coding structure based on one profit centre and three cost centres as outlined in the first four columns of the table below. Each code has a sub-code so each transaction will be coded as ***/***

**You are required to classify the revenue and expense transactions shown in the transaction column of the table below using the code column for your answer.**

| Profit/Cost centre | Cost code | Sub-classification | Sub-code | Transaction | Code |
|---|---|---|---|---|---|
| Sales | 120 | Sportswear | 075 | | |
| | | Leisurewear | 085 | | |
| Production | 230 | Direct cost | 160 | Sales of football shirts | |
| | | Indirect cost | 170 | Cotton used in leisure shirts | |
| Administration | 340 | Direct cost | 255 | Cleaning materials used in factory | |
| | | Indirect cost | 265 | Sales of casual shorts | |
| Selling and Distribution | 450 | Direct cost | 340 | Heating of administration offices | |
| | | Indirect cost | 350 | Cost of advertising campaign | |

## Task 5 (6 marks)

Firstglow Ltd has set up an investment centre for a project it is undertaking over a period of years. It uses an alpha coding system for its investments, revenues and costs and then further classifies numerically as outlined in the first four columns of the table below.

**You are required to code the transactions listed in the transaction column of the table below using the code column for your answers. Each transaction should have a five character code.**

| Activity | Code | Nature of cost | Sub-code | | Transaction | Code |
|---|---|---|---|---|---|---|
| Investments | IN | External | 210 | | External funds used to set up investment | |
| | | Internal | 240 | | External contractor charge | |
| Revenues | RE | UK | 320 | | Material used on project | |
| | | Overseas | 350 | | Salaries paid to employees | |
| Costs | CO | Material | 420 | | Project revenue arising in the UK | |
| | | Labour | 530 | | Firstglow Ltd company funds invested in project | |
| | | Overheads | 640 | | | |

## Task 6 (9 marks)

(a) **Identify the type of cost behaviour (fixed, variable or semi-variable) described in each statement by putting a tick in the relevant column of the table below.**

| Statement | Fixed | Variable | Semi-variable |
|---|---|---|---|
| Costs of £2 per unit at 20,000 units and £10 per unit at 4,000 units | ☐ | ☐ | ☐ |
| Costs of £30,000 are made up of a fixed charge of £10,000 and a further cost of £5 per unit at 4,000 units | ☐ | ☐ | ☐ |
| Costs are £25,000 units at 10,000 units and £40,000 at 16,000 units | ☐ | ☐ | ☐ |

(b) **Classify the following costs as either fixed or variable by putting a tick in the relevant column of the table below.**

| Costs | Fixed | Variable |
|---|---|---|
| Materials used in the production of a product | ☐ | ☐ |
| Employees paid on a time-rate basis for an agreed number of hours per week | ☐ | ☐ |
| Annual Health and Safety inspection | ☐ | ☐ |

## Task 7 (9 marks)

The table below lists a number of costs

(a) **Indicate whether the following costs are an overhead or not by putting a tick in the relevant column of the table below.**

| Cost | Yes | No |
|---|---|---|
| Fee paid to an external accountant | ☐ | ☐ |
| Salary of chief executive | ☐ | ☐ |
| Wages of production workers making the product | ☐ | ☐ |

Havenport Ltd makes a single product. A production level of 75,000 units has the following costs:

Materials  50,000 kilos at £33 per kilo
Labour    40,000 hours at £22.50 per hour
Overheads  £1,950,000

(b) **Complete the table below to show the unit product cost at the production level of 75,000 units.**

| Element | Unit Product Cost £ |
|---|---|
| Materials | |
| Labour | |
| Direct Cost | |
| Overheads | |
| Total | |

## Task 8 (14 marks)

(a) **Re-order the following costs into a manufacturing account format for the year ended 31 December. You should write each item in the position where you want it to be on the list on the right side of the page below.**

| Costs | £ | Manufacturing account | £ |
|---|---|---|---|
| MANUFACTURING COST | | | |
| Direct labour | 144,000 | | |
| COST OF GOODS SOLD | | | |
| COST OF GOODS MANUFACTURED | | | |
| Closing inventory of finished goods | 101,200 | | |
| DIRECT COST | | | |
| Opening inventory of raw materials | 52,700 | | |
| Closing inventory of raw materials | 48,100 | | |
| Closing inventory of work in progress | 74,200 | | |
| Manufacturing overheads | 237,400 | | |
| DIRECT MATERIALS USED | | | |
| Opening inventory of finished goods | 107,600 | | |
| Opening inventory of work in progress | 72,400 | | |
| Purchase of raw materials | 221,100 | | |

(b) **Enter the correct figures for the following costs which were not provided in part (a).**

| Manufacturing account | £ |
|---|---|
| DIRECT MATERIALS USED | |
| DIRECT COST | |
| MANUFACTURING COST | |
| COST OF GOODS MANUFACTURED | |
| COST OF GOODS SOLD | |

## Task 9 (9 marks)

You are told the opening inventory of a single raw material in the stores is 1,200 units at £6.00 per unit. During the month 1,800 units at £8.00 per unit are received and the following week 2,400 units are issued.

(a) **Identify the valuation method described in the statements below.**

| Statement | FIFO | LIFO | AVCO |
|---|---|---|---|
| The closing inventory is valued at £4,800 | ☐ | ☐ | ☐ |
| The issue of 2,400 units is costed at £17,280 | ☐ | ☐ | ☐ |
| The issue of 2,400 units is costed at £18,000 | ☐ | ☐ | ☐ |

You are told the opening inventory of a single raw material in the stores is 1,200 units at £6.00 per unit. During the month 1,800 units at £8.00 per unit are received and the following week 2,400 units are issued.

(b) **Identify whether the statements in the table below are true or false by putting a tick in the relevant column.**

| Statement | True | False |
|---|---|---|
| AVCO values the closing inventory at £4,320 | ☐ | ☐ |
| FIFO costs the issue of 2,400 units at £16,900 | ☐ | ☐ |
| LIFO values the closing inventory at £3,600 | ☐ | ☐ |

## Task 10 (9 marks)

A business has the following movements in a certain type of inventory into and out of its stores for the month of February.

| DATE | RECEIPTS | | ISSUES | |
|---|---|---|---|---|
| | Units | Cost | Units | Cost |
| Feb 4 | 1,000 | £4,000 | | |
| Feb 7 | 500 | £2,500 | | |
| Feb 11 | 2,000 | £11,000 | | |
| Feb 19 | | | 2,100 | |
| Feb 24 | 1,800 | £11,700 | | |

Complete the table below by entering the cost of issue and closing inventory values.

| Method | Cost of issue on 19 February (£) | Closing inventory at 28 February (£) |
|---|---|---|
| FIFO | | |
| LIFO | | |
| AVCO | | |

## Task 11 (8 marks)

An employee is paid £8.00 an hour and is expected to make 25 units an hour.

Any excess production will be paid a bonus of 20p per unit.

(a) **Identify the following statements as being true or false by putting a tick in the relevant column of the table below.**

| Statements | True | False |
|---|---|---|
| During a 36 hour week an employee produces 910 units and does not receive a bonus | ☐ | ☐ |
| During a 40 hour week an employee produces 1,180 units and receives a bonus of £36 | ☐ | ☐ |
| During a 37 hour week an employee produces 980 units and receives total pay of £307 | ☐ | ☐ |

Northcake Ltd pays a time-rate of £12.50 per hour for a 36 hour week.

Any employee working in excess of 36 hours per week is paid an overtime rate of £15.00 per hour.

(b) **Calculate the basic wage, overtime and gross wage for the week for the two employees in the table below. Note: if no overtime is paid you should enter 0 as the overtime for that employee.**

| Employee | Hours worked | Basic wage £ | Overtime £ | Gross wage £ |
|---|---|---|---|---|
| V. Chopra | 40 | | | |
| R. Silvai | 43 | | | |

## Task 12 (8 marks)

Piecework is a method of paying labour.

**Identify the following statements about the piecework method as either true or false by putting a tick in the relevant column of the table below.**

| Statement | True | False |
|---|---|---|
| Employees' pay will increase if more units are produced | ☐ | ☐ |
| An employee is paid 45p per unit and earns £288 for a production of 640 units | ☐ | ☐ |
| An employee who is paid £350 for a production of 875 units is paid 40p per unit | ☐ | ☐ |
| Employees paid on a piecework basis will always earn an agreed total amount of pay | ☐ | ☐ |

## Task 13 (9 marks)

Fanfest Ltd uses a time-rate method with bonus to pay the employees in its factory. The time-rate used is £11.00 per hour and an employee is expected to produce 12 units per hour; anything over this and the employee is paid a bonus of 25p per unit.

**Calculate the basic wage, bonus and gross wage for the week for the three employees in the table below. Note: if no bonus is paid you should enter 0 as the bonus for that employee in the table.**

| Employee | Hours worked | Units produced | Basic wage £ | Bonus £ | Gross wage £ |
|---|---|---|---|---|---|
| L. Singh | 42 | 500 | | | |
| M. Barton | 39 | 540 | | | |
| S. Valencia | 41 | 508 | | | |

## Task 14 (12 marks)

Westley Ltd makes a single product and has the following income and expenditure data:

Sales Revenue £8 per unit
Variable Costs £5 per unit
Fixed Costs £10,000 per month

The number of units sold by Westley during the last three months is as follows:

January 2,000 units
February 4,000 units
March 5,000 units

The spreadsheet below has been partly formatted in order to provide income and expenditure information for the three months.

(a) **Complete the formatting of the spreadsheet by selecting column headings from the picklist. Complete the rows for February, March and Total by inserting figures in the cells.**

| | A | B | C | D | E | F |
|---|---|---|---|---|---|---|
| 1 | | ▼ | Fixed Cost £ | ▼ | Sales Revenue £ | ▼ |
| 2 | January | 10,000 | 10,000 | 20,000 | 16,000 | (4,000) |
| 3 | February | | | | | |
| 4 | March | | | | | |
| 5 | Total | | | | | |

**Picklist:**

Fixed Costs £
Profit/(Loss) £
Sales Revenue £
Total Costs £
Variable Costs £

(b) **Insert the formulas in the table below that you used for row 5 of columns B, C, D and F. (Note: column E is not required.)**

| | A | B | C | D | E | F |
|---|---|---|---|---|---|---|
| 5 | | | | | | |

## Task 15 (8 marks)

Listed below are four statements about spreadsheets.

**Identify the statements as being true or false by putting a tick in the relevant column of the table below.**

| Statement | True | False |
|---|---|---|
| A cell is used to enter data | ☐ | ☐ |
| A formula cannot be used in a spreadsheet | ☐ | ☐ |
| A password is used as the title of a worksheet | ☐ | ☐ |
| A worksheet is used to record and analyse data | ☐ | ☐ |

## Task 16 (12 marks)

Johnson Ltd has the following actual results for the month of April which are to be compared to the budget:

Income      £40,000

Expenditure:

Materials    £15,000
Labour       £8,000
Overheads  £7,500

(a) **Enter the above data into the spreadsheet below, calculate the variance for each item of income and expenditure, and determine whether it is adverse or favourable (enter A or F).**

| | A | B | C | D | E |
|---|---|---|---|---|---|
| 1 | Income/Expenditure | Budget £ | Actual £ | Variance £ | Adverse or Favourable (A or F) |
| 2 | Income | 45,000 | | | |
| 3 | Material | 15,800 | | | |
| 4 | Labour | 9,000 | | | |
| 5 | Overheads | 8,800 | | | |

(b) **Insert the formulas in the table below that you used for cells, 2, 3, 4 and 5 of <u>column D</u> of the spreadsheet.**

| | D |
|---|---|
| 1 | Variance £ |
| 2 | |
| 3 | |
| 4 | |
| 5 | |

## Task 17 (8 marks)

Below is an extract of the spreadsheet for Johnson Ltd for last month.

|  | A | B | C | D |
|---|---|---|---|---|
| 1 | Income/Expenditure | Budget £ | Variance £ | Adverse (A) or Favourable (F) |
|  | Income | 45,000 | 1,500 | F |
|  | Material | 15,800 | 3,900 | A |
|  | Labour | 9,000 | 890 | F |
|  | Overheads | 8,800 | 1,700 | A |

(a) Identify how the spreadsheet would look if it were re-ordered using the data from column C in descending order. Rewrite the spreadsheet in that order.

|  | A | B | C | D |
|---|---|---|---|---|
| 1 | Income/Expenditure | Budget £ | Variance £ | Adverse (A) or Favourable (F) £ |
| 2 | ▼ |  |  |  |
| 3 | ▼ |  |  |  |
| 4 | ▼ |  |  |  |
| 5 | ▼ |  |  |  |

**Picklist:**

Income
Material
Labour
Overheads

**Select from the list below the variance that appears in cell C3.**

| 1,500 | ☐ |
|---|---|
| 3,900 | ☐ |
| 890 | ☐ |
| 1,700 | ☐ |

The following spreadsheet shows budgeted income and variances for last month for Johnson Ltd. It is company policy to provide managers with a variance report highlighting significant variances.

Any variance in excess of 10% is considered significant.

(b) **In column E, identify significant variances in excess of 10% of budget, entering S for significant and NS for <u>not</u> significant.**

| | A | B | C | D | E |
|---|---|---|---|---|---|
| 1 | Income/Expenditure £ | Budget £ | Variance £ | Adverse (A) or Favourable (F) | Significant (S) o Not Significant (N |
| 2 | Income | 45,000 | 1,500 | F | |
| 3 | Material | 15,800 | 3,900 | A | |
| 4 | Labour | 9,000 | 890 | F | |
| 5 | Overheads | 8,800 | 1,700 | A | |

# AAT AQ2013 SAMPLE ASSESSMENT
# BASIC COSTING

# ANSWERS

# AAT Sample Assessment: Basic Costing

## Task 1 (8 marks)

(a)

| Statement | True | False |
|---|---|---|
| FIFO is a technique used to cost issues and to value inventories | ✓ | ☐ |
| The piecework method to pay labour guarantees a set amount of wages | ☐ | ✓ |
| A variance calculation measures the difference between revenue and cost | ✓ | ✓ |
| Classification of cost by behaviour allows the planning of total cost at differing levels of output | ✓ | ☐ |

(b)

| Characteristic | Financial Accounting | Management Accounting |
|---|---|---|
| This system produces statements that are used as a basis to determine the tax charge | ✓ | ☐ |
| This system uses techniques to cost issues and to value inventories | ☐ | ✓ |
| This system produces statements that are primarily for internal use | ☐ | ✓ |
| This system produces statements that have many external users | ✓ | ☐ |

## Task 2 (8 marks)

(a)

| Cost | Material | Labour | Overhead |
|---|---|---|---|
| Insurance of office computers | ☐ | ☐ | ✓ |
| Ink cartridges used in the production of pens | ✓ | ☐ | ☐ |
| Wages of employees in the production department | ☐ | ✓ | ☐ |
| Card used to produce binders for notebooks | ✓ | ☐ | ☐ |

(b)

| Cost | Direct | Indirect |
|---|---|---|
| Insurance of factory | ☐ | ✓ |
| Paper used in the manufacture of envelopes | ✓ | ☐ |
| Salary of production manager | ☐ | ✓ |
| Plastic used in the production of pens | ✓ | ☐ |

## Task 3 (8 marks)

(a)

| Cost | Production | Administration | Selling and distribution | Finance |
|---|---|---|---|---|
| Fruit purchased for use in drinks | ✓ | | | |
| Stationery provided to all departments | | ✓ | | |
| Interest charged on bank loan | | | | ✓ |
| Sales campaign | | | ✓ | |

(b)

| Cost | Fixed | Variable | Semi-variable |
|---|---|---|---|
| Employees in the bottling department paid on a piecework basis | | ✓ | |
| Annual consultancy charge for updating the website | ✓ | | |
| Sugar used in drinks | | ✓ | |
| Machinery hire consisting of a fixed rental charge and a usage charge | | | ✓ |

## Task 4 (6 marks)

| Profit/Cost centre | Cost code | Sub-classification | Sub-code | | Transaction | Code |
|---|---|---|---|---|---|---|
| Sales | 120 | Sportswear | 075 | | | |
| | | Leisurewear | 085 | | | |
| Production | 230 | Direct cost | 160 | | Sales of football shirts | 120/075 |
| | | Indirect cost | 170 | | Cotton used in leisure shirts | 230/160 |
| Administration | 340 | Direct cost | 255 | | Cleaning materials used in factory | 230/170 |
| | | Indirect cost | 265 | | Sales of casual shorts | 120/085 |
| Selling and Distribution | 450 | Direct cost | 340 | | Heating of administration offices | 340/265 |
| | | Indirect cost | 350 | | Cost of advertising campaign | 450/350 |

## Task 5 (6 marks)

| Activity | Code | Nature of cost | Sub-code | | Transaction | Code |
|---|---|---|---|---|---|---|
| Investments | IN | External | 210 | | External funds used to set up investment | IN210 |
| | | Internal | 240 | | External contractor charge | CO640 |
| Revenues | RE | UK | 320 | | Material used on project | CO420 |
| | | Overseas | 350 | | Salaries paid to employees | CO530 |
| Costs | CO | Material | 420 | | Project revenue arising in the UK | RE320 |
| | | Labour | 530 | | Firstglow Ltd company funds invested in project | IN240 |
| | | Overheads | 640 | | | |

# Task 6 (9 marks)

(a)

| Statement | Fixed | Variable | Semi-variable |
|---|:---:|:---:|:---:|
| Costs of £2 per unit at 20,000 units and £10 per unit at 4,000 units (working 1) | ✓ | ☐ | ☐ |
| Costs of £30,000 are made up of a fixed charge of £10,000 and a further cost of £5 per unit at 4,000 units | ☐ | ☐ | ✓ |
| Costs are £25,000 units at 10,000 units and £40,000 at 16,000 units (working 2) | ☐ | ✓ | ☐ |

**Workings:**

1    20,000 × £2 = £40,000; 4,000 × £10 = £40,000. Therefore this is a fixed cost

2    £25,000/10,000 = £2.50 per unit; £40,000/16,000 = £2.50 per unit. Therefore this is a variable cost

(b)

| Costs | Fixed | Variable |
|---|:---:|:---:|
| Materials used in the production of a product | ☐ | ✓ |
| Employees paid on a time-rate basis for an agreed number of hours per week | ✓ | ☐ |
| Annual Health and Safety inspection | ✓ | ☐ |

## Task 7 (9 marks)

(a)

| Cost | Yes | No |
|---|:---:|:---:|
| Fee paid to an external accountant | ✓ | ☐ |
| Salary of chief executive | ✓ | ☐ |
| Wages of production workers making the product | ☐ | ✓ |

(b) **Unit product cost at the production level of 75,000 units.**

| Element | Unit Product Cost £ |
|---|:---:|
| Materials | 22 |
| Labour | 12 |
| Direct Cost | 34 |
| Overheads | 26 |
| Total | 60 |

**Workings:**

Materials: $(50,000 \times £33)/75,000 = £22$ per unit of product

Labour: $(40,000 \times £22.50)/75,000 = £12$ per unit of product

Overheads: $£1,950,000/75,000 = £26$ per unit

# Task 8 (14 marks)

(a)

| Costs | £ | Manufacturing account | £ |
|---|---|---|---|
| MANUFACTURING COST | | Opening inventory of raw materials | 52,700 |
| Direct labour | 144,000 | Purchase of raw materials | 221,100 |
| COST OF GOODS SOLD | | Closing inventory of raw materials | 48,100 |
| COST OF GOODS MANUFACTURED | | DIRECT MATERIALS USED | |
| Closing inventory of finished goods | 101,200 | Direct labour | 144,000 |
| DIRECT COST | | DIRECT COST | |
| Opening inventory of raw materials | 52,700 | Manufacturing overheads | 237,400 |
| Closing inventory of raw materials | 48,100 | MANUFACTURING COST | |
| Closing inventory of work in progress | 74,200 | Opening inventory of work in progress | 72,400 |
| Manufacturing overheads | 237,400 | Closing inventory of work in progress | 74,200 |
| DIRECT MATERIALS USED | | COST OF GOODS MANUFACTURED | |
| Opening inventory of finished goods | 107,600 | Opening inventory of finished goods | 107,600 |
| Opening inventory of work in progress | 72,400 | Closing inventory of finished goods | 101,200 |
| Purchase of raw materials | 221,100 | COST OF GOODS SOLD | |

.............................................................................

(b)

| Manufacturing account | £ |
|---|---|
| DIRECT MATERIALS USED | 225,700 |
| DIRECT COST | 369,700 |
| MANUFACTURING COST | 607,100 |
| COST OF GOODS MANUFACTURED | 605,300 |
| COST OF GOODS SOLD | 611,700 |

.............................................................................

## Task 9 (9 marks)

(a)

| Statement | FIFO | LIFO | AVCO |
|---|---|---|---|
| The closing inventory is valued at £4,800 | ✓ | ☐ | ☐ |
| The issue of 2,400 units is costed at £17,280 | ☐ | ☐ | ✓ |
| The issue of 2,400 units is costed at £18,000 | ☐ | ✓ | ☐ |

(b)

| Statement | True | False |
|---|---|---|
| AVCO values the closing inventory at £4,320 | ✓ | ☐ |
| FIFO costs the issue of 2,400 units at £16,900 | ☐ | ✓ |
| LIFO values the closing inventory at £3,600 | ✓ | ☐ |

**Workings:**

| | Units | Per unit £ | Total £ | Balance £ |
|---|---|---|---|---|
| Opening inventory | 1,200 | 6 | 7,200 | 7,200 |
| Received | 1,800 | 8 | 14,400 | 21,600 |
| | 3,000 | | | |
| Issued | (2,400) | | | |
| Closing inventory | 600 | | | |

| | FIFO | LIFO | AVCO |
|---|---|---|---|
| Issue | (1,200 × £6) + (1,200 × £8) = £16,800 | (600 × £6) + (1,800 × £8) = £18,000 | 2,400 × £21,600/3,000 = £17,280 |
| Closing inventory | 600 × £8 = £4,800 | 600 × £6 = £3,600 | 600 × £21,600/3,000 = £4,320 |

# Task 10 (9 marks)

| Method | Cost of issue on 19 February (£) | Closing inventory at 28 February (£) |
|---|---|---|
| FIFO | 9,800 | 19,400 |
| LIFO | 11,500 | 17,700 |
| AVCO | 10,500 | 18,700 |

**Workings:**

| | Units | Per unit £ | Total £ | Balance £ |
|---|---|---|---|---|
| Feb 4 Receipt | 1,000 | 4 | 4,000 | 4,000 |
| Feb 7 Receipt | 500 | 5 | 2,500 | 6,500 |
| Feb 11 Receipt | 2,000 | 5.50 | 11,000 | 17,500 |
| | 3,500 | | | |
| Feb 19 Issue | (2,100) | | | |
| | 1,400 | | | |
| Feb 24 Receipt | 1,800 | 6.50 | 11,700 | |
| Feb 24 Closing inventory | 3,200 | | | |

| | FIFO | LIFO | AVCO |
|---|---|---|---|
| Issue | (1,000 × £4) + (500 × £5) + (600 × £5.50) = £9,800 | (2,000 × £5.50) + (100 × £5) = £11,500 | 2,100 × £17,500/3,500 = £10,500 |
| Closing inventory | (1,400 × £5.50) + £11,700 = £19,400 | (1,000 × £4) + (400 × £5) + £11,700 = £17,700 | £17,500 – £10,500 + £11,700 = £18,700 |

## Task 11 (8 marks)

(a)

| Statements | True | False |
|---|---|---|
| During a 36 hour week an employee produces 910 units and does not receive a bonus | ☐ | ✓ |
| During a 40 hour week an employee produces 1,180 units and receives a bonus of £36 | ✓ | ☐ |
| During a 37 hour week an employee produces 980 units and receives total pay of £307 | ✓ | ☐ |

### Workings

1  Expected output: 36 × 25 = 900 units. Producing 910 items means the employee DOES receive a bonus

2  Expected output: 40 × 25 = 1,000 units, producing 180 extra units results in a bonus of 180 × £0.20 = £36

3  Expected output: 37 × 25 = 925 units. Total pay: (37 × £8) + ((980 – 925) × £0.20) = £307

(b)

| Employee | Hours worked | Basic wage £ | Overtime £ | Gross wage £ |
|---|---|---|---|---|
| V. Chopra | 40 | 450.00 | 60.00 | 510.00 |
| R. Silvai | 43 | 450.00 | 105.00 | 555.00 |

### Workings:

| | Basic £ | Overtime £ |
|---|---|---|
| V. Chopra | 36 × £12.50 | 4 × £15.00 |
| R, Silvai | 36 × £12.50 | 7 × £15.00 |

## Task 12 (8 marks)

| Statement | True | False |
|---|:---:|:---:|
| Employees' pay will increase if more units are produced | ✓ | ☐ |
| An employee is paid 45p per unit and earns £288 for a production of 640 units | ✓ | ☐ |
| An employee who is paid £350 for a production of 875 units is paid 40p per unit | ✓ | ☐ |
| Employees paid on a piecework basis will always earn an agreed total amount of pay | ☐ | ✓ |

**Workings:**

2    640 × £0.45 = £288

3    £350/875 = £0.40 per unit

## Task 13 (9 marks)

| Employee | Hours worked | Units produced | Basic wage £ | Bonus £ | Gross wage £ |
|---|---|---|---|---|---|
| L. Singh | 42 | 500 | 462.00 | 0 | 462.00 |
| M. Barton | 39 | 540 | 429.00 | 18.00 | 447.00 |
| S. Valencia | 41 | 508 | 451.00 | 4.00 | 455.00 |

**Workings:**

| | Basic £ | Expected output | Bonus £ |
|---|---|---|---|
| L. Singh | 42 × £11 | 42 × 12 = 504 units | (500 − 504) × £0.25 = 0 |
| M. Barton | 39 × £11 | 39 × 12 = 468 units | (540 − 468) × £0.25 = £18.00 |
| S. Valencia | 41 × £11 | 41 × 12 = 492 units | (508 − 492) × £0.25 = £4.00 |

## Task 14 (12 marks)

(a)

|   | A | B | C | D | E | F |
|---|---|---|---|---|---|---|
| 1 | | Variable Costs £ | Fixed Cost £ | Total Costs £ | Sales Revenue £ | Profit/(Loss £ |
| 2 | January | 10,000 | 10,000 | 20,000 | 16,000 | (4,000) |
| 3 | February | 20,000 | 10,000 | 30,000 | 32,000 | 2,000 |
| 4 | March | 25,000 | 10,000 | 35,000 | 40,000 | 5,000 |
| 5 | Total | 55,000 | 30,000 | 85,000 | 88,000 | 3,000 |

(b)

|   | A | B | C | D | E | F |
|---|---|---|---|---|---|---|
| 5 | | =SUM(B2:B4) Or =(B2+B3+B4) | =SUM(C2:C4) Or =(C2+C3+C4) | =SUM(D2:D4) Or =(D2+D3+D4) Or =(B5+C5) | | =SUM(F2:F4) Or =(F2+F3+F4) Or =(E5-D5) |

## Task 15 (8 marks)

| Statement | True | False |
|---|---|---|
| A cell is used to enter data | ✓ | |
| A formula cannot be used in a spreadsheet | | ✓ |
| A password is used as the title of a worksheet | | ✓ |
| A worksheet is used to record and analyse data | ✓ | |

## Task 16 (12 marks)

(a)

| | A | B | C | D | E |
|---|---|---|---|---|---|
| 1 | Income/Expenditure | Budget £ | Actual £ | Variance £ | Adverse or Favourable (A or F) |
| 2 | Income | 45,000 | 40,000 | 5,000 | A |
| 3 | Material | 15,800 | 15,000 | 800 | F |
| 4 | Labour | 9,000 | 8,000 | 1,000 | F |
| 5 | Overheads | 8,800 | 7,500 | 1,300 | F |

(b)

| | D |
|---|---|
| 1 | Variance £ |
| 2 | =(B2-C2) |
| 3 | =(B3-C3) |
| 4 | =(B4-C4) |
| 5 | =(B5-C5) |

## Task 17 (8 marks)

(a)

| | A | B | C | D |
|---|---|---|---|---|
| 1 | Income/Expenditure | Budget £ | Variance £ | Adverse (A) or Favourable (F) £ |
| 2 | Material | 15,800 | 3,900 | A |
| 3 | Overheads | 8,800 | 1,700 | A |
| 4 | Income | 45,000 | 1,500 | F |
| 5 | Labour | 9,000 | 890 | F |

1,500   ☐

3,900   ☐

890   ☐

1,700   ☑

(b)

| | A | B | C | D | E |
|---|---|---|---|---|---|
| 1 | Income/Expenditure £ | Budget £ | Variance £ | Adverse (A) or Favourable (F) | Significant (S) Not Significant ( |
| 2 | Income | 45,000 | 1,500 | F | NS |
| 3 | Material | 15,800 | 3,900 | A | S |
| 4 | Labour | 9,000 | 890 | F | NS |
| 5 | Overheads | 8,800 | 1,700 | A | S |

# BPP PRACTICE ASSESSMENT 1
# BASIC COSTING

**Time allowed: 2 hours**

PRACTICE ASSESSMENT 1

# Basic Costing BPP practice assessment 1

## Task 1

(a) Costing uses an number of techniques to assist management.

**Identify the following statements as being True or False by putting a tick in the relevant column of the table below.**

| Statement | True | False |
|---|---|---|
| When a time-rate system is used to pay employees, pay remains the same even when output fluctuates due to demand | | |
| All variances between budget and actual costs and income should be treated as significant and be fully investigated | | |
| When a piecework system of pay is used, less efficient workers are paid the same as more efficient ones | | |
| An adverse variance means budgeted costs are lower than actual costs | | |
| AVCO costs issues of inventory at the oldest purchase price | | |

(b) The table below lists some of the characteristics of manufacturing, retail and service organisations.

**Indicate a characteristic for each organisation by putting a tick in the relevant column of the table below.**

| Characteristic | Retail | Manufacturing | Service |
|---|---|---|---|
| Does not make or sell a physical product | | | |
| Buys in ready-made goods to sell | | | |
| Buys in raw materials | | | |

## Task 2

(a) Dartmouth Ltd is a manufacturer of garden gnomes.

**Classify the following costs it incurred by element (materials, labour or overheads) by putting a tick in the relevant column of the table below.**

| Cost | Materials | Labour | Overhead |
|------|-----------|--------|----------|
| Salary of the accounts manager | | | |
| Wages of employees painting the gnomes | | | |
| Electricity in the workshops | | | |
| Plaster used in making the gnomes | | | |

(b) Totnes Ltd is in business as a beauty salon.

**Classify the following costs by nature (direct or indirect) by putting a tick in the relevant column of the table below.**

| Cost | Direct | Indirect |
|------|--------|----------|
| Wages of beauticians | | |
| Wages of security guard | | |
| Rent and rates for salon | | |
| Nail polish used on nails | | |

## Task 3

(a) Barnstaple Ltd produces surfboards.

**Classify the following costs by function (production, administration, selling and distribution or finance) by putting a tick in the relevant column of the table below.**

| Cost | Production | Administration | Selling and Distribution | Finance |
|---|---|---|---|---|
| Purchases of fibreglass for the boards | | | | |
| Cost of delivering finished boards to surf shops | | | | |
| Fee paid to re-arrange overdraft facility | | | | |
| Salaries of board waxers | | | | |
| Fees for monthly bookkeeper | | | | |

(b) Exmouth Ltd is a manufacturer of tweed cloth.

**Classify the following costs by their behaviour (fixed, variable, or semi-variable) by putting a tick in the relevant column of the table below.**

| Cost | Fixed | Variable | Semi-variable |
|---|---|---|---|
| Labour costs paid on a piecework basis | | | |
| Spun wool used in making the cloth | | | |
| Marketing cost for the year | | | |
| Telephone costs for the sales staff that include a standing charge | | | |

## Task 4

Torbay Limited offers two services for dogs: kennel care and dog grooming. It uses a numeric coding system for its one profit centre (sales) and three cost centres (operations, administration, and distribution) as outlined in the table below. Each code has a sub-code so each transaction will be coded as **/***.

| Element of cost | Cost code | Sub-classification | Sub-code |
|---|---|---|---|
| Sales | 10 | Kennel care | 100 |
| | | Grooming | 200 |
| Operations | 30 | Direct cost | 100 |
| | | Indirect cost | 200 |
| Administration | 50 | Direct cost | 100 |
| | | Indirect cost | 200 |
| Distribution | 70 | Direct cost | 100 |
| | | Indirect cost | 200 |

**You are required to classify the income and expense transactions shown in the transaction column of the table below using the code column for your answer.**

| Transaction | Code |
|---|---|
| Shampoo used in grooming | |
| Fees for solicitors to negotiate rent reduction on parlour | |
| Salary of kennel maid | |
| Wages of driver | |
| Fees received for keeping dogs in kennels | |

## Task 5

Bovey Ltd has set up a new division as an investment centre to make and sell tractors. It uses an alpha-numerical coding structure for investments, revenues and costs and then further classifies transactions numerically. This is outlined in the table below.

| Activity | Code | Nature of transaction | Sub-code |
|---|---|---|---|
| Investments | AB | Assets | 100 |
| | | Liabilities | 200 |
| Revenues | LM | Large | 100 |
| | | Small | 200 |
| Costs | XY | Materials | 100 |
| | | Labour | 200 |
| | | Overheads | 300 |

You are required to code the following transactions using the table below. Each code should have five characters in the format *****.

| Transaction | Code |
|---|---|
| Paint for tractors | |
| Sales of small tractors | |
| Factory rates | |
| Machinery purchased for factory | |
| Salary of factory supervisor | |
| Loan taken out to pay for the machinery | |

## Task 6

(a) **Identify the following statements as either True or False by putting a tick in the relevant column of the table below.**

| | True | False |
|---|---|---|
| Fixed costs never change | | |
| Variable costs change with output levels | | |
| Semi-variable costs show a step increase at a particular level of output | | |

(b) Plustyre Ltd fixes cars and makes sure they are valeted so they are returned to their owners in a perfect state.

**Classify the following costs as either fixed or variable by putting a tick in the relevant column of the table below.**

| Costs | Fixed | Variable |
|---|---|---|
| Valets paid at piecework rate for each car valeted | | |
| Hourly wages of mechanics paid for each car fixed | | |
| Salaries of supervisors | | |
| Rent for the workshop used to fix cars | | |

## Task 7

(a) **Identify the following statements as True or False by putting a tick in the relevant column of the table below.**

|  | True | False |
|---|---|---|
| The variable cost per unit rises with the level of output |  |  |
| Overheads vary in line with output |  |  |

(b) Kingswear Ltd makes a single product and for a production level of 20,000 units has the following cost details:

| Materials | 5,000 kilos at | £10 per kilo |
|---|---|---|
| Labour | 4,000 hours at | £15 an hour |
| Overheads |  | £50,000 |

**Complete the table below to show the unit product cost at the production level of 20,000 units.**

| Element | Unit product cost £ |
|---|---|
| Material |  |
| Labour |  |
| Direct cost |  |
| Overheads |  |
| Total |  |

# Task 8

(a) Reorder all the following costs into a manufacturing account format for the year ended 31 December. You should write out each item, including figures, in the position where you want it to be on the list on the right side of the table below.

| | £ | £ |
|---|---|---|
| Closing inventory of work in progress | 25,000 | |
| Direct labour | 242,500 | |
| Opening inventory of raw materials | 17,500 | |
| Closing inventory of finished goods | 62,500 | |
| Closing inventory of raw materials | 25,000 | |
| Manufacturing overheads | 132,500 | |
| COST OF GOODS SOLD | | |
| MANUFACTURING COST | | |
| Purchases of raw materials | 125,000 | |
| Opening inventory of work in progress | 20,000 | |
| Opening inventory of finished goods | 75,000 | |
| DIRECT COST | | |
| DIRECT MATERIALS USED | | |
| COST OF GOODS MANUFACTURED | | |

(b) Enter the correct figures for the following costs which were not provided in part (a).

| | £ |
|---|---|
| DIRECT MATERIALS USED | |
| DIRECT COST | |
| MANUFACTURING COST | |
| COST OF GOODS MANUFACTURED | |
| COST OF GOODS SOLD | |

## Task 9

You are told the opening inventory of a good purchased for resale is 1,500 units at £9 per unit. In week 2 of the month further purchases were made of 1,000 at £10 per unit. In week 3, 500 units were issued from stores.

(a) **Identify the valuation method described in the statements below.**

| Characteristic | FIFO | LIFO | AVCO |
|---|---|---|---|
| The issue of 500 units is costed at £5,000 | | | |
| Closing inventory is valued at £18,800 | | | |
| Closing inventory is valued at £19,000 | | | |

(b) **Identify whether each of the following statements is True or False by putting a tick in the relevant column.**

| Statement | True | False |
|---|---|---|
| AVCO values the issue at £4,700 | | |
| FIFO costs the issue at £4,800 | | |
| LIFO values the closing inventory at £18,500 | | |

## Task 10

Jersey Ltd has the following movements in a certain type of inventory into and out of its stores for the month of May:

| DATE | RECEIPTS | | ISSUES | |
|------|----------|------|--------|------|
| | Units | Cost | Units | Cost |
| May 5 | 500 | £1,500 | | |
| May 8 | 750 | £3,000 | | |
| May 12 | 1,250 | £6,250 | | |
| May 18 | | | 1,500 | |
| May 25 | 1,000 | £6,000 | | |

Complete the table below for the issue and closing inventory values.

| Method | Cost of issue on 18 May £ | Closing inventory at 31 May £ |
|--------|----------------------------|-------------------------------|
| FIFO | | |
| LIFO | | |
| AVCO | | |

## Task 11

(a) **Identify whether each of the following statements describes the time-rate method of paying employees by putting a tick in the relevant column.**

| Payment method | Time-rate method | NOT time-rate method |
|---|---|---|
| An amount is paid to the employee for each unit or task successfully completed | | |
| A basic amount is paid per hour worked | | |
| If output exceeds a preset level an incentive is paid in addition to basic pay | | |

(b) Cardiff Ltd pays a time-rate of £15 per hour to its direct labour for a standard 35-hour week. Any of the labour force working in excess of 35 hours is paid an overtime rate of £25 per hour.

**Calculate the gross wage for the week for the two workers in the table below.**

| Worker | Hours worked | Basic wage £ | Overtime £ | Gross wage £ |
|---|---|---|---|---|
| J Edwards | 35 hours | | | |
| L Rakowski | 41 hours | | | |

## Task 12

Swansea Ltd uses a piecework method to pay labour in one of its factories. The rate used is 70p per unit produced.

**Calculate the gross wage for the week for the two workers in the table below.**

| Worker | Units produced in week | Gross wage £ |
|---|---|---|
| G Gently | 350 units | |
| A Ransome | 390 units | |

## Task 13

Brecon Ltd uses a time-rate method with bonus to pay its direct labour in one of its factories. The time-rate used is £15 per hour and a worker is expected to produce five units an hour, anything over this and the worker is paid a bonus of £1.50 per unit.

**Calculate the basic wage, bonus and gross wage for the week for the three workers in the table below.**

| Worker | Hours worked | Units produced | Basic wage £ | Bonus £ | Gross wage £ |
|---|---|---|---|---|---|
| R Butler | 35 | 160 | | | |
| S Douglas | 35 | 155 | | | |
| L Howard | 35 | 200 | | | |

## Task 14

Jones Ltd makes a single product and has the following income and expenditure data:

Sales revenue    £10.00 per unit

Variable costs    £7.50 per unit

Fixed costs    £30,000 per month

The number of units sold by Jones Ltd in the last three months is as follows:

March 15,000 units

April   11,000 units

May    18,000 units

The spreadsheet below has been partly formatted in order to provide income and expenditure information for the three months.

(a) **Complete the formatting of the spreadsheet by selecting column headings from the picklist. Insert figures in the cells for April, May and Total.**

|   | A | B | C | D | E | F |
|---|---|---|---|---|---|---|
| 1 | | Variable cost £ | ▼ | ▼ | Sales revenue £ | ▼ |
| 2 | March | 112,500 | 30,000 | 142,500 | 150,000 | 7,500 |
| 3 | April | | | | | |
| 4 | May | | | | | |
| 5 | Total | | | | | |

**Picklist:**

Total cost £
Variable cost £
Profit/(loss) £
Sales revenue £
Fixed cost £

(b) **Insert the formulas in the table below that you need for cells B5, C5, D5 and F5.**

|   | A | B | C | D | E | F |
|---|---|---|---|---|---|---|
| 5 | | | | | | |

## Task 15

Listed below are four statements about spreadsheets.

**Identify whether each statement is true or false by putting a tick in the relevant column.**

| Statement | True | False |
|---|---|---|
| A worksheet can contain any number of spreadsheets, like a book can contain any number of pages | | |
| Since a spreadsheet is computer software, information is calculated automatically and does not need to be checked before being presented to managers | | |
| Formulae can be used in a spreadsheet to make calculations involving data contained in it | | |
| A spreadsheet should be saved securely | | |

## Task 16

Torre Ltd has the following actual results for the month of November, which it wishes to compare with the November budget.

Income        £80,000:

Costs

Materials                £15,000

Labour                   £25,000

Overheads                £12,000

(a) **Enter the above data into the spreadsheet below, calculate the variance for each item of income and cost, and determine indicate whether it is adverse of favourable using the picklist.**

| | A | B | C | D | E |
|---|---|---|---|---|---|
| 1 | | Budget £ | Actual £ | Variance £ | Adverse or Favourable |
| 2 | Income | 78,500 | | | ▼ |
| 3 | Materials | 16,000 | | | ▼ |
| 4 | Labour | 23,200 | | | ▼ |
| 5 | Overheads | 10,000 | | | ▼ |

**Picklist:**

Adverse
Favourable

● ● ● ● ● ● ● ● ● ● ● ● ● ● ● ● ● ● ● ● ● ● ● ● ● ● ● ● ● ● ● ● ● ● ● ● ● ● ● ● ● ● ● ● ● ● ● ● ● ● ● ● ● ● ● ● ● ● ● ● ● ● ● ● ● ● ● ● ● ● ● ● ● ● ● ● ● ●

(b) **Insert the formulas in the table below that you used for cells D2, D3, D4 and D5 of the spreadsheet**

|   | D |
|---|---|
| 1 | Variance £ |
| 2 | |
| 3 | |
| 4 | |
| 5 | |

● ● ● ● ● ● ● ● ● ● ● ● ● ● ● ● ● ● ● ● ● ● ● ● ● ● ● ● ● ● ● ● ● ● ● ● ● ● ● ● ● ● ● ● ● ● ● ● ● ● ● ● ● ● ● ● ● ● ● ● ● ● ● ● ● ● ● ● ● ● ● ● ● ● ● ● ● ●

# Task 17

(a) A spreadsheet has been prepared for Bryce Ltd for last year as follows.

|   | A | B | D | E |
|---|---|---|---|---|
| 1 | | Budget £ | Variance £ | Adverse or Favourable |
| 2 | Income | 250,000 | 5,000 | Favourable |
| 3 | Materials | 46,000 | 7,200 | Adverse |
| 4 | Labour | 33,600 | 2,400 | Adverse |
| 5 | Overheads | 17,800 | 1,900 | Favourable |

To re-order rows 2 to 5 of the spreadsheet so that the variances in column C are presented in ascending order of size, which sort button would you use? Answer yes or no for each button by placing a tick in the relevant column.

|   | Yes | No |
|---|---|---|
| A Z ↓ Sort | | |
| Z A ↓ Sort | | |

When the rows are sorted correctly, which variance would appear in cell D5? Tick ONE box.

| Variance £ | Appears in cell D5 |
|---|---|
| 5,000 | |
| 7,200 | |
| 2,400 | |
| 1,900 | |

(b) The following spreadsheet shows budgeted costs plus variances for last month for Dahl Ltd. It is company policy to provide managers with a variance report highlighting significant variances, which is any variance of 10% or more

Indicate whether each variance is significant or not significant by using the picklist.

| | A | B | C | D | E |
|---|---|---|---|---|---|
| 1 | | Budget £ | Variance £ | Adverse/ Favourable | Significant/ Not significan |
| 2 | Direct materials | 35,000 | 3,335 | Adverse | |
| 3 | Direct labour | 70,000 | 8,015 | Adverse | |
| 4 | Production overheads | 65,000 | 4,208 | Favourable | |
| 5 | Administration overheads | 54,000 | 5,980 | Adverse | |
| 6 | Selling and distribution overheads | 42,000 | 1,150 | Adverse | |

**Picklist:**

Significant

Not significant

BPP
LEARNING MEDIA

# BPP PRACTICE ASSESSMENT 1
# BASIC COSTING

# ANSWERS

# Basic Costing BPP practice assessment 1

## Task 1

(a)

| Statement | True | False |
|---|---|---|
| When a time-rate system is used to pay employees, pay remains the same even when output fluctuates due to demand | ✓ | |
| All variances between budget and actual costs and income should be treated as significant and be fully investigated | | ✓ |
| When a piecework system of pay is used, less efficient workers are paid the same as more efficient ones | | ✓ |
| An adverse variance means budgeted costs are lower than actual costs | ✓ | |
| AVCO costs issues of inventory at the oldest purchase price | | ✓ |

(b)

| Characteristic | Retail | Manufacturing | Service |
|---|---|---|---|
| Does not make or sell a physical product | | | ✓ |
| Buys in ready-made goods to sell | ✓ | | |
| Buys in raw materials | | ✓ | |

## Task 2

(a)

| Cost | Materials | Labour | Overheads |
|---|---|---|---|
| Salary of the accounts manager | | | ✓ |
| Wages of employees painting the gnomes | | ✓ | |
| Electricity in the workshops | | | ✓ |
| Plaster used in making the gnomes | ✓ | | |

(b)

| Cost | Direct | Indirect |
|------|--------|----------|
| Wages of beauticians | ✓ | |
| Wages of security guard | | ✓ |
| Rent and rates for salon | | ✓ |
| Nail polish used on nails | ✓ | |

## Task 3

(a)

| Cost | Production | Administration | Selling and Distribution | Financ |
|------|-----------|----------------|--------------------------|--------|
| Purchases of fibreglass for the boards | ✓ | | | |
| Cost of delivering finished boards to surf shops | | | ✓ | |
| Fee paid to re-arrange overdraft facility | | | | ✓ |
| Salaries of board waxers | ✓ | | | |
| Fees for monthly bookkeeper | | ✓ | | |

(b)

| Cost | Fixed | Variable | Semi-variable |
|------|-------|----------|---------------|
| Labour costs paid on a piecework basis | | ✓ | |
| Spun wool used in making the cloth | | ✓ | |
| Marketing cost for the year | ✓ | | |
| Telephone costs for the sales staff that include a standing charge | | | ✓ |

# Task 4

| Transaction | Code |
|---|---|
| Shampoo used in grooming | 30/100 |
| Fees for solicitors to negotiate rent reduction on parlour | 50/200 |
| Salary of kennel maid | 30/100 |
| Wages of driver | 70/200 |
| Fees received for keeping dogs in kennels | 10/100 |

# Task 5

| Transaction | Code |
|---|---|
| Paint for tractors | XY100 |
| Sales of small tractors | LM200 |
| Factory rates | XY300 |
| Machinery purchased for factory | AB100 |
| Salary of factory supervisor | XY200 |
| Loan taken out to pay for the machinery | AB200 |

# Task 6

(a)

| | True | False |
|---|---|---|
| Fixed costs never change | | ✓ |
| Variable costs change with output levels | ✓ | |
| Semi-variable costs show a step increase at a particular level of output | | ✓ |

(b)

| Costs | Fixed | Variable |
|---|:---:|:---:|
| Valets paid at piecework rate for each car valeted | | ✓ |
| Hourly wages of mechanics paid for each car fixed | | ✓ |
| Salaries of supervisors | ✓ | |
| Rent for the workshop used to fix cars | ✓ | |

## Task 7

(a)

| | True | False |
|---|:---:|:---:|
| The variable cost per unit rises with the level of output | | ✓ |
| Overheads vary in line with output | | ✓ |

(b)

| Element | Unit product cost £ |
|---|:---:|
| Material | 2.50 |
| Labour | 3.00 |
| Direct cost | 5.50 |
| Overheads | 2.50 |
| Total | 8.00 |

# Task 8

(a)

| | £ | | £ |
|---|---|---|---|
| Closing inventory of work in progress | 25,000 | Opening inventory of raw materials | 17,500 |
| Direct labour | 242,500 | Purchases of raw materials | 125,000 |
| Opening inventory of raw materials | 17,500 | Closing inventory of raw materials | 25,000 |
| Closing inventory of finished goods | 62,500 | DIRECT MATERIALS USED | |
| Closing inventory of raw materials | 25,000 | Direct labour | 242,500 |
| Manufacturing overheads | 132,500 | DIRECT COST | |
| COST OF GOODS SOLD | | Manufacturing overheads | 132,500 |
| MANUFACTURING COST | | MANUFACTURING COST | |
| Purchases of raw materials | 125,000 | Opening inventory of work in progress | 20,000 |
| Opening inventory of work in Progress | 20,000 | Closing inventory of work in Progress | 25,000 |
| Opening inventory of finished goods | 75,000 | COST OF GOODS MANUFACTURED | |
| DIRECT COST | | Opening inventory of finished goods | 75,000 |
| DIRECT MATERIALS USED | | Closing inventory of finished goods | 62,500 |
| COST OF GOODS MANUFACTURED | | COST OF GOODS SOLD | |

(b)

|  | £ |
|---|---|
| DIRECT MATERIALS USED | 117,500 |
| DIRECT COST | 360,000 |
| MANUFACTURING COST | 492,500 |
| COST OF GOODS MANUFACTURED | 487,500 |
| COST OF GOODS SOLD | 500,000 |

## Task 9

(a)

| Characteristic | FIFO | LIFO | AVCO |
|---|---|---|---|
| The issue of 500 units is costed at £5,000 |  | ✓ |  |
| Closing inventory is valued at £18,800 |  |  | ✓ |
| Closing inventory is valued at £19,000 | ✓ |  |  |

(b)

| Statement | True | False |
|---|---|---|
| AVCO values the issue at £4,700 | ✓ |  |
| FIFO costs the issue at £4,800 |  | ✓ |
| LIFO values the closing inventory at £18,500 | ✓ |  |

120

| Workings | Units | Per unit £ | Total £ | Balance £ |
|---|---|---|---|---|
| Opening inventory | 1,500 | 9 | 13,500 | 13,500 |
| Received | 1,000 | 10 | 10,000 | 23,500 |
| | 2,500 | | | |
| Issued | (500) | | | |
| Closing inventory | 2,000 | | | |

| | FIFO | LIFO | AVCO |
|---|---|---|---|
| Issue | 500 × £9 = £4,500 | 500 × £10 = £5,000 | 500 × £23,500/2,500 = £4,700 |
| Inventory | (1,000 × £9) + (1,000 × £10) = £19,000 | (1,500 × £9) + (500 × £10) = £18,500 | 2,000 × £23,500/2,500 = £18,800 |

# Task 10

| Method | Cost of issue on 18 May | Closing inventory at 31 May |
|---|---|---|
| FIFO | 1,500 + 3,000 + (250/1,250 × 6,250) = **£5,750** | 6,000 + (1,000/1,250 × 6,250) = **£11,000** |
| LIFO | 6,250 + (250/750 × 3,000) = **£7,250** | 1,500 + (500/750 × 3,000) + 6,000 = **£9,500** |
| AVCO | [(1,500 + 3,000 + 6,250)/2,500 ]× 1,500 = **£6,450** | [(1,500 + 3,000 + 6,250)/2,500] × 1,000 + 6,000 = **£10,300** |

# Task 11

(a)

| Payment method | Time-rate method | NOT time-rate method |
|---|---|---|
| An amount is paid to the employee for each unit or task successfully completed | | ✓ |
| A basic amount is paid per hour worked | ✓ | |
| If output exceeds a preset level an incentive is paid in addition to basic pay | | ✓ |

(b)

| Worker | Hours worked | Basic wage £ | Overtime £ | Gross wage £ |
|---|---|---|---|---|
| J Edwards | 35 hours | 525 | 0 | 525 |
| L Rakowski | 41 hours | 525 | 150 | 675 |

## Task 12

| Worker | Units produced in week | Gross wage £ |
|---|---|---|
| G Gently | 350 units | 245 |
| A Ransome | 390 units | 273 |

## Task 13

| Worker | Hours worked | Units produced | Basic wage £ | Bonus £ | Gross wage £ |
|---|---|---|---|---|---|
| R Butler | 35 | 160 | 525.00 | 0.00 | 525.00 |
| S Douglas | 35 | 155 | 525.00 | 0.00 | 525.00 |
| L Howard | 35 | 200 | 525.00 | 37.50 | 562.50 |

## Task 14

(a)

| | A | B | C | D | E | F |
|---|---|---|---|---|---|---|
| 1 | | Variable cost £ | Fixed cost £ | Total cost £ | Sales revenue £ | Profit/(loss) £ |
| 2 | March | 112,500 | 30,000 | 142,500 | 150,000 | 7,500 |
| 3 | April | 82,500 | 30,000 | 112,500 | 110,000 | (2,500) |
| 4 | May | 135,000 | 30,000 | 165,000 | 180,000 | 15,000 |
| 5 | Total | 330,000 | 90,000 | 420,000 | 440,000 | 20,000 |

(b)

| | A | B | C | D | E | F |
|---|---|---|---|---|---|---|
| 5 | | =SUM(B2:B4) or =(B2+B3+B4) | =SUM(C2:C4) or =(C2+C3+C4) | =SUM(D2:D4) or =(D2+D3+D4) Or =(B5+C5) | | =SUM(F2:F4) or =(F2+F3+F4) Or =(E5-D5) |

## Task 15

| Statement | True | False |
|---|---|---|
| A worksheet can contain any number of spreadsheets, like a book can contain any number of pages | | ✓ |
| Since a spreadsheet is computer software, information is calculated automatically and does not need to be checked before being presented to managers | | ✓ |
| Formulae can be used in a spreadsheet to make calculations involving data contained in it | ✓ | |
| A spreadsheet should be saved securely | ✓ | |

## Task 16

(a)

| | A | B | C | D | E |
|---|---|---|---|---|---|
| 1 | | Budget £ | Actual £ | Variance £ | Adverse or Favourable |
| 2 | Income | 78,500 | 80,000 | 1,500 | Favourable |
| 3 | Materials | 16,000 | 15,000 | 1,000 | Favourable |
| 4 | Labour | 23,200 | 25,000 | 1,800 | Adverse |
| 5 | Overheads | 10,000 | 12,000 | 2,000 | Adverse |

(b)

| | D |
|---|---|
| 1 | Variance £ |
| 2 | =(B2-C2) |
| 3 | =(B3-C3) |
| 4 | =(B4-C4) |
| 5 | =(B5-C5) |

## Task 17

(a)

| | Yes | No |
|---|---|---|
| A Z Sort | ✓ | |
| Z A Sort | | ✓ |

| Variance £ | Appears in cell D5 |
|---|---|
| 5,000 | |
| 7,200 | ✓ |
| 2,400 | |
| 1,900 | |

(b)

| | A | B | C | D | E |
|---|---|---|---|---|---|
| 1 | | Budget £ | Variance £ | Adverse/ Favourable | Significant/ Not significant |
| 2 | Direct materials | 35,000 | 3,335 | Adverse | Not significant |
| 3 | Direct labour | 70,000 | 8,015 | Adverse | Significant |
| 4 | Production overheads | 65,000 | 4,208 | Favourable | Not significant |
| 5 | Administration overheads | 54,000 | 5,980 | Adverse | Significant |
| 6 | Selling and Distribution overheads | 42,000 | 1,150 | Adverse | Not significant |

# BPP PRACTICE ASSESSMENT 2
# BASIC COSTING

**Time allowed: 2 hours**

# Basic Costing – BPP practice assessment 2

## Task 1

(a) **Identify whether the following statements are True or False by putting a tick in the relevant column of the table below.**

|  | True | False |
|---|---|---|
| If prices of materials are rising  FIFO will give a higher inventory valuation than LIFO |  |  |
| A variance is the difference between budgeted and expected cost |  |  |
| In a LIFO system the most recent purchases are issued first |  |  |
| Financial accounting results in the presentation of financial information for external users |  |  |

(b) The table below lists some typical business transactions.

**Indicate whether each one is capital or revenue by putting a tick in the relevant column.**

| Transaction | Capital | Revenue |
|---|---|---|
| Purchase of office furniture for office manager |  |  |
| Purchase of office furniture by office furniture saleroom for resale |  |  |
| Paying VAT |  |  |
| Making cash sales |  |  |

## Task 2

(a)  Ambleside Ltd makes walking boots.

**Classify the following costs by element (materials, labour or overheads) by putting a tick in the relevant column of the table below.**

| Cost | Materials | Labour | Overheads |
|---|---|---|---|
| Rent and rates on the workshop | | | |
| Leather for making the boots | | | |
| Salary of bookkeeper employed in the business | | | |
| Wages of two cobblers making lasts for the boots | | | |

(b)  Windermere Ltd is in business as a health spa and resort hotel.

**Classify the following costs by nature (direct or indirect) by putting a tick in the relevant column of the table below.**

| Cost | Direct | Indirect |
|---|---|---|
| Supplies of food bought in for the kitchen | | |
| Interest on mortgage to buy the hotel | | |
| Hotel cashier's salary | | |
| Wages of waiters in the hotel restaurant | | |

## Task 3

(a) Derwentwater Ltd makes dinghies.

Classify the following costs by function (production, administration, selling and distribution or finance) by putting a tick in the relevant column of the table below.

| Cost | Production | Administration | Selling and Distribution | Finance |
|---|---|---|---|---|
| Advertising dinghies in local newspaper | | | | |
| Material for making sails in the factory | | | | |
| Fees to estate agent for locating new premises | | | | |
| Interest charged on long-term loan | | | | |

(b) Bassenthwaite Ltd is a pottery making bowls and cups.

Classify the following costs by their behaviour (fixed, variable, or semi-variable) by putting a tick in the relevant column of the table below.

| Cost | Fixed | Variable | Semi-variable |
|---|---|---|---|
| Charge for electricity for the kilns firing the pots that includes a standing charge | | | |
| Annual entertainment budget for the pottery | | | |
| Cost of glazes bought in to glaze the pots | | | |
| Labour costs for potters paid on a piecework basis | | | |

## Task 4

Cockermouth Limited operates a chain of bakeries and uses an alpha-numeric coding system for its elements of cost (materials, labour or overheads) and then further classifies each element by nature (direct or indirect cost) as below. So, for example, the code for direct materials is M100.

| Element of cost | Code | Nature of cost | Code |
|---|---|---|---|
| Materials | M | Direct | 100 |
| | | Indirect | 200 |
| Labour | L | Direct | 100 |
| | | Indirect | 200 |
| Overheads | O | Direct | 100 |
| | | Indirect | 200 |

**Code the following costs, extracted from invoices and payroll, using the table below.**

| Cost | Code |
|---|---|
| Wages of delivery driver | |
| Fees for annual audit by local accountants | |
| Yeast used in baking | |
| Bakers' salaries | |
| Wood used to fuel special pizza oven | |

BPP
LEARNING MEDIA

## Task 5

Carlisle Ltd makes drills for use by dentists. It uses a numeric coding structure based on one profit centre and three cost centres as outlined below. Each code has a sub-code so each transaction will be coded as **/**.

| Profit/Cost centre | Code | Sub-classification | Sub-code |
|---|---|---|---|
| Sales | 10 | Power drill sales | 25 |
| | | Laser drill sales | 55 |
| Production | 20 | Direct cost | 35 |
| | | Indirect cost | 65 |
| Administration | 30 | Direct cost | 45 |
| | | Indirect cost | 75 |
| Selling and Distribution | 40 | Direct cost | 80 |
| | | Indirect cost | 90 |

**Code the following revenue and expense transactions, which have been extracted from purchase invoices, sales invoices and payroll, using the table below.**

| Transaction | Code |
|---|---|
| Rent paid on the workshop | |
| Electricity for payroll/HR offices | |
| Sales of laser drills | |
| Sales of power drills | |
| Steel for drill heads | |
| Sales representatives' wages | |

## Task 6

(a) **Identify the following statements as either True or False by putting a tick in the relevant column of the table below.**

|  | True | False |
|---|---|---|
| Fixed costs are also known as period costs and generally remain the same however many units are produced |  |  |
| Variable costs change directly with changes in activity |  |  |
| If a cost is £15 per unit at output of 3,000 units and £5 per unit when output is 9,000 units, the cost is a fixed cost |  |  |

(b) **Classify the following costs as either fixed or variable by putting a tick in the relevant column of the table below.**

| Costs | Fixed | Variable |
|---|---|---|
| Chemicals used in making paint |  |  |
| Wages of machine operators paid at a piecework rate |  |  |
| Salaries of maintenance workers |  |  |
| Business rates on a car showroom |  |  |

## Task 7

(a) **Identify whether the following costs should be treated as overheads by putting a tick in the relevant column of the table below.**

|  | Yes | No |
|---|---|---|
| Depreciation on vehicles operated by the sales force |  |  |
| Flour used to bake bread |  |  |
| Wages of management accountant |  |  |

(b) **Gretna Ltd makes a single product and for a production level of 10,000 units has the following cost details:**

Materials 10,000 kilos at   £10 per kilo
Labour 8,000 hours at   £20 an hour
Overheads   £40,000

**Complete the table below to show the unit cost at the production level of 10,000 units.**

| Element | Unit cost at 10,000 units £ |
|---|---|
| Materials | |
| Labour | |
| Direct cost | |
| Overheads | |
| Total | |

# Task 8

(a) **Reorder the following headings and costs into a manufacturing account format on the right side of the table below for the year ended 30 September.**

| Cost | £ | Manufacturing account | £ |
|---|---|---|---|
| MANUFACTURING COST | | | |
| Closing inventory of work in progress | 12,500 | | |
| Closing inventory of finished goods | 31,250 | | |
| Opening inventory of raw materials | 8,750 | | |
| Closing inventory of raw materials | 12,500 | | |
| DIRECT MATERIALS USED | | | |
| Manufacturing overheads | 66,250 | | |
| COST OF GOODS SOLD | | | |
| Direct labour | 121,250 | | |
| COST OF GOODS MANUFACTURED | | | |
| Purchases of raw materials | 62,500 | | |
| DIRECT COST | | | |
| Opening inventory of work in progress | 10,000 | | |
| Opening inventory of finished goods | 37,500 | | |

(b) **Enter the correct figures for the following costs which were not provided in part (a).**

| Manufacturing account | £ |
|---|---|
| DIRECT MATERIALS USED | |
| DIRECT COST | |
| MANUFACTURING COST | |
| COST OF GOODS MANUFACTURED | |
| COST OF GOODS SOLD | |

## Task 9

You are told the opening inventory of a single good for resale in the warehouse is 2,000 units at £20.00 per unit. During the month 3,000 units at £22.00 per unit are received and the following week 3,200 units are issued for sale.

(a) **Identify the valuation method described in the statements below.**

| Statement | FIFO | LIFO | AVCO |
|---|---|---|---|
| The closing inventory is valued at £36,000 | | | |
| The issue of 3,200 units is costed at £67,840 | | | |
| The closing inventory is valued at £39,600 | | | |

You are told the opening inventory of a single good for resale in the warehouse is 2,000 units at £20.00 per unit. During the month 3,000 units at £22.00 per unit are received and the following week 3,200 units are issued for sale.

(b) **Identify whether the statements in the table below are true or false by putting a tick in the relevant column.**

| Statement | True | False |
|---|---|---|
| AVCO values the closing inventory at £38,120 | | |
| FIFO costs the issue of 3,200 units at £66,400 | | |
| LIFO costs the issue of 3,200 units at £70,000 | | |

## Task 10

Jersey Ltd has the following movements in a certain type of inventory into and out of its stores for the month of July:

| DATE | RECEIPTS | | ISSUES | |
|---|---|---|---|---|
| | Units | Cost £ | Units | Cost £ |
| July 5 | 1,000 | 1,500 | | |
| July 8 | 1,500 | 3,000 | | |
| July 12 | 2,500 | 6,250 | | |
| July 20 | | | 3,000 | |
| July 25 | 2,000 | 6,000 | | |

**Complete the table below for the issue and closing inventory values.**

| Method | Cost of issue on 20 July £ | Closing inventory at 31 July £ |
|---|---|---|
| FIFO | | |
| LIFO | | |
| AVCO | | |

## Task 11

(a) **Identify each labour payment method by putting a tick in the relevant column of the table below.**

| Payment method | Time-rate | Piecework | Piecework plus bonus |
|---|---|---|---|
| This method acts as an incentive to produce more | | | |
| A basic amount is paid per hour worked | | | |
| If output is better than expected a bonus is paid | | | |

(b) Exeter Ltd pays a time-rate of £12.50 per hour to its direct labour for a standard 35-hour week. Any of the labour force working in excess of 35 hours is paid an overtime rate of £15 per hour.

**Calculate the gross wage for the week for the two workers in the table below.**

| Worker | Hours worked | Basic wage £ | Overtime £ | Gross wage £ |
|---|---|---|---|---|
| J Collins | 35 hours | | | |
| M Thatcher | 40 hours | | | |

## Task 12

Axminster Ltd uses a piecework method to pay labour in one of its factories. The rate used is 80p per unit produced.

**Calculate the gross wage for the week for the two workers in the table below.**

| Worker | Units produced in week | Gross wage £ |
|---|---|---|
| A Daley | 375 units | |
| G Cole | 435 units | |

## Task 13

Seaton Ltd uses a time-rate method with bonus to pay its direct labour in one of its factories. The time-rate used is £10.50 per hour and a worker is expected to produce six units an hour, anything over this and the worker is paid a bonus of £1.25 per unit.

**Calculate the gross wage for the week including bonus for the three workers in the table below.**

| Worker | Hours worked | Units produced | Basic wage £ | Bonus £ | Gross wage £ |
|---|---|---|---|---|---|
| M Rochester | 35 | 180 | | | |
| J Eyre | 35 | 195 | | | |
| A Grey | 35 | 230 | | | |

## Task 14

Watson Ltd makes a single product and has the following production and cost data:

Variable Costs     £10 per unit
Fixed Costs        £20,000 per month

Watson Ltd can choose to produce 500, 2,500, 5,000 or 7,500 units over its next budget period. It wishes to identify its unit cost at each level of production.

The spreadsheet below has been partly formatted in order to provide expenditure information for the three months.

(a) **Complete the formatting of the spreadsheet by selecting column headings from the picklist. Complete rows 3, 4 and 5 by inserting figures in the cells, correct to two decimal places.**

|   | A | B | C | D | E |
|---|---|---|---|---|---|
| 1 | Units produced | [ ▼ ] | Variable Costs £ | [ ▼ ] | Unit cost £ |
| 2 | 500 | 20,000 | 5,000 | 25,000 | 50.00 |
| 3 |   |   |   |   |   |
| 4 |   |   |   |   |   |
| 5 |   |   |   |   |   |

**Picklist:**

Fixed Costs £
Unit cost £
Units produced
Total Costs £
Variable Costs £

...........................................................................................

(b) **Insert the formulas in the table below that you used for rows 3, 4 and 5 of column E.**

|   | E |
|---|---|
| 3 |   |
| 4 |   |
| 5 |   |

...........................................................................................

## Task 15

Listed below are four statements about spreadsheets.

**Identify the statements as being true or false by putting a tick in the relevant column of the table below.**

| Statement | True | False |
|---|---|---|
| To show a figure as a percentage in a cell, it must be formatted as such | | |
| Only numerical data can be keyed into a spreadsheet | | |
| Re-ordering a spreadsheet can be achieved by sorting data in ascending or descending order | | |
| Spreadsheets are automatically secure so no password is required | | |

## Task 16

(a) Colyton Ltd has the following actual results for the month of February which are to be compared to the budget:

Income          £139,125

Expenditure:

Direct materials      £20,200
Direct labour          £56,125
Production overheads      £32,120

**Enter the above data into the spreadsheet below, calculate the amount of each variance and then determine whether it is adverse or favourable by typing F for favourable and A for adverse in the right-hand column of the table below.**

| | A | B | C | D | E |
|---|---|---|---|---|---|
| 1 | Cost type | Budget £ | Actual £ | Variance £ | Adverse (A)/ Favourable (F) |
| 2 | Income | 136,500 | | | |
| 3 | Direct materials | 25,500 | | | |
| 4 | Direct labour | 55,000 | | | |
| 5 | Production overheads | 35,000 | | | |

(b) **Insert the formulas in the table below that you used for cells 2, 3, 4 and 5 of <u>column D</u> of the spreadsheet.**

| | D |
|---|---|
| 1 | Variance £ |
| 2 | |
| 3 | |
| 4 | |
| 5 | |

## Task 17

(a) The following performance report for this month has been produced for Weston Ltd as a spreadsheet. Any variance in excess of 5% of budget is deemed to be significant and should be reported to the relevant manager for review and appropriate action.

**Calculate each variance as a percentage of the budgeted amount, correct to one decimal place. Indicate whether each variance is significant or not significant by inserting S or NS.**

| | A | B | C | D | E | F |
|---|---|---|---|---|---|---|
| 1 | Cost type | Budget £ | Variance £ | Adverse/ Favourable | Variance as percentage of budget % | Significant (S)/ Not significant (NS) |
| 2 | Direct materials | 170,000 | 8,750 | Adverse | | |
| 3 | Direct labour | 140,000 | 9,025 | Adverse | | |
| 4 | Production overheads | 52,000 | 4,218 | Favourable | | |
| 5 | Administration overheads | 45,000 | 5,810 | Adverse | | |
| 6 | Selling and Distribution overheads | 22,000 | 500 | Adverse | | |

(b) **Insert the formulas in the table below that you used for cells 2, 3, 4, 5 and 6 of <u>column E</u> of the spreadsheet.**

| | E |
|---|---|
| 1 | Variance as percentage of budget % |
| 2 | =(C2/B2) |
| 3 | =(C3/B3) |
| 4 | =(C4/B4) |
| 5 | =(C5/B5) |
| 6 | =(C6/B6) |

# BPP PRACTICE ASSESSMENT 2
# BASIC COSTING

# ANSWERS

# Basic Costing BPP practice assessment 2

## Task 1

### (a)

|  | True | False |
|---|---|---|
| If prices of materials are rising FIFO will give a higher inventory valuation than LIFO |  | ✓ |
| A variance is the difference between budgeted and expected cost |  | ✓ |
| In a LIFO system the most recent purchases are issued first | ✓ |  |
| Financial accounting results in the presentation of financial information for external users | ✓ |  |

### (b)

| Transaction | Capital | Revenue |
|---|---|---|
| Purchase of office furniture for office manager | ✓ |  |
| Purchase of office furniture by office furniture saleroom for resale |  | ✓ |
| Paying VAT |  | ✓ |
| Making cash sales |  | ✓ |

## Task 2

### (a)

| Cost | Materials | Labour | Overheads |
|---|---|---|---|
| Rent and rates on the workshop |  |  | ✓ |
| Leather for making the boots | ✓ |  |  |
| Salary of bookkeeper employed in the business |  |  | ✓ |
| Wages of two cobblers making lasts for the boots |  | ✓ |  |

(b)

| Cost | Direct | Indirect |
|------|--------|----------|
| Supplies of food bought in for the kitchen | ✓ | |
| Interest on mortgage to buy the hotel | | ✓ |
| Hotel cashier's salary | | ✓ |
| Wages of waiters in the hotel restaurant | ✓ | |

## Task 3

(a)

| Cost | Production | Administration | Selling and Distribution | Finance |
|------|-----------|----------------|--------------------------|---------|
| Advertising dinghies in local newspaper | | | ✓ | |
| Material for making sails in the factory | ✓ | | | |
| Fees to estate agent for locating new premises | | ✓ | | |
| Interest charged on long-term loan | | | | ✓ |

(b)

| Cost | Fixed | Variable | Semi-variable |
|------|-------|----------|---------------|
| Charge for electricity for the kilns firing the pots that includes a standing charge | | | ✓ |
| Annual entertainment budget for the pottery | ✓ | | |
| Cost of glazes bought in to glaze the pots | | ✓ | |
| Labour costs for potters paid on a piecework basis | | ✓ | |

## Task 4

| Cost | Code |
|---|---|
| Wages of delivery driver | L200 |
| Fees for annual audit by local accountants | O200 |
| Yeast used in baking | M100 |
| Bakers' salaries | L100 |
| Wood used to fuel special pizza oven | M200 |

## Task 5

| Transaction | Code |
|---|---|
| Rent paid on the workshop | 20/65 |
| Electricity for payroll/HR offices | 30/75 |
| Sales of laser drills | 10/55 |
| Sales of power drills | 10/25 |
| Steel for drill heads | 20/35 |
| Sales representatives' wages | 40/90 |

## Task 6

(a)

| | True | False |
|---|---|---|
| Fixed costs are also known as period costs and generally remain the same however many units are produced | ✓ | |
| Variable costs change directly with changes in activity | ✓ | |
| If a cost is £15 per unit at output of 3,000 units and £5 per unit when output is 9,000 units, the cost is a fixed cost | ✓ | |

(b)

| Costs | Fixed | Variable |
|---|---|---|
| Chemicals used in making paint | | ✓ |
| Wages of machine operators paid at a piecework rate | | ✓ |
| Salaries of maintenance workers | ✓ | |
| Business rates on a car showroom | ✓ | |

## Task 7

(a)

| | Yes | No |
|---|---|---|
| Depreciation on vehicles operated by the sales force | ✓ | |
| Flour used to bake bread | | ✓ |
| Wages of management accountant | ✓ | |

(b)

| Element | Unit cost at 10,000 units £ |
|---|---|
| Materials | 10.00 |
| Labour | 16.00 |
| Direct cost | 26.00 |
| Overheads | 4.00 |
| Total | 30.00 |

# Task 8

(a)

## Manufacturing Account   Y/e 30 September

|  | £ |
|---|---|
| Opening inventory of raw materials | 8,750 |
| Purchases of raw materials | 62,500 |
| Closing inventory of raw materials | 12,500 |
| DIRECT MATERIALS USED |  |
| Direct labour | 121,250 |
| DIRECT COST |  |
| Manufacturing overheads | 66,250 |
| MANUFACTURING COST |  |
| Opening inventory of work in progress | 10,000 |
| Closing inventory of work in progress | 12,500 |
| COST OF GOODS MANUFACTURED |  |
| Opening inventory of finished goods | 37,500 |
| Closing inventory of finished goods | 31,250 |
| COST OF GOODS SOLD |  |

(b)

| Manufacturing account | £ |
|---|---|
| DIRECT MATERIALS USED | 58,750 |
| DIRECT COST | 180,000 |
| MANUFACTURING COST | 246,250 |
| COST OF GOODS MANUFACTURED | 243,750 |
| COST OF GOODS SOLD | 250,000 |

# Task 9

(a)

| Statement | FIFO | LIFO | AVCO |
|---|---|---|---|
| The closing inventory is valued at £36,000 | | ✓ | |
| The issue of 3,200 units is costed at £67,840 | | | ✓ |
| The closing inventory is valued at £39,600 | ✓ | | |

(b)

| Statement | True | False |
|---|---|---|
| AVCO values the closing inventory at £38,120 | | ✓ |
| FIFO costs the issue of 3,200 units at £66,400 | ✓ | |
| LIFO costs the issue of 3,200 units at £70,000 | ✓ | |

## Workings:

| | Units | Per unit £ | Total £ | Balance £ |
|---|---|---|---|---|
| Opening inventory | 2,000 | 20 | 40,000 | 40,000 |
| Received | 3,000 | 22 | 66,000 | 106,000 |
| | 5,000 | | | |
| Issued | (3,200) | | | |
| Closing inventory | 1,800 | | | |

| | FIFO | LIFO | AVCO |
|---|---|---|---|
| Issue | (2,000 × £20) + (1,200 × £22) = £66,400 | (3,000 × £22) + (200 × £20) = £70,000 | 3,200 × £106,000/5,000 = £67,840 |
| Closing inventory | 1,800 × £22 = £39,600 | (1,800 × £20) = £36,000 | 1,800 × £106,000/5,000 = £38,160 |

# Task 10

| Method | Cost of issue on 20 July £ | Closing inventory at 31 July £ |
|---|---|---|
| FIFO | £1,500 + £3,000 +(500/2,500 × £6,250) = **£5,750** | £6,000 + (2,000/2,500 × £6,250) = **£11,000** |
| LIFO | £6,250 + (500/1,500 × £3,000) = **£7,250** | £6,000 + £1,500 + (1,000/1,500 × £3,000) = **£9,500** |
| AVCO | [(£1,500 + £3,000 + £6,250)/5,000] × 3,000 = **£6,450** | £6,000 + [(£1,500 + £3,000 + £6,250)/5,000 × 2,000] = **£10,300** |

# Task 11

(a)

| Payment method | Time-rate | Piecework | Piecework plus bonus |
|---|---|---|---|
| This method acts as an incentive to produce more | | ✓ | |
| A basic amount is paid per hour worked | ✓ | | |
| If output is better than expected a bonus is paid | | | ✓ |

(b)

| Worker | Hours worked | Basic wage £ | Overtime £ | Gross wage £ |
|---|---|---|---|---|
| J Collins | 35 hours | 437.50 | 0 | 437.50 |
| M Thatcher | 40 hours | 437.50 | 75.00 | 512.50 |

## Task 12

| Worker | Units produced in week | Gross wage £ |
|---|---|---|
| A Daley | 375 units | 300 |
| G Cole | 435 units | 348 |

## Task 13

| Worker | Hours worked | Units produced | Basic wage £ | Bonus £ | Gross wage £ |
|---|---|---|---|---|---|
| M Rochester | 35 | 180 | 367.50 | 0 | 367.50 |
| J Eyre | 35 | 195 | 367.50 | 0 | 367.50 |
| A Grey | 35 | 230 | 367.50 | 25.00 | 392.50 |

## Task 14

(a)

| | A | B | C | D | E |
|---|---|---|---|---|---|
| 1 | Units produced | Fixed Costs £ | Variable Costs £ | Total Costs £ | Unit cost £ |
| 2 | 500 | 20,000 | 5,000 | 25,000 | 50.00 |
| 3 | 2,500 | 20,000 | 25,000 | 45,000 | 18.00 |
| 4 | 5,000 | 20,000 | 50,000 | 70,000 | 14.00 |
| 5 | 7,500 | 20,000 | 75,000 | 95,000 | 12.67 |

(b) **Insert the formulas in the table below that you used for rows 3, 4 and 5 of column E.**

|   | E |
|---|---|
| 3 | =(D3/A3) |
| 4 | =(D4/A4) |
| 5 | =(D5/A5) |

## Task 15

| Statement | True | False |
|---|---|---|
| To show a figure as a percentage in a cell, it must be formatted as such | ✓ | |
| Only numerical data can be keyed into a spreadsheet | | ✓ |
| Re-ordering a spreadsheet can be achieved by sorting data in ascending or descending order | ✓ | |
| Spreadsheets are automatically secure so no password is required | | ✓ |

## Task 16

(a)

|   | A | B | C | D | E |
|---|---|---|---|---|---|
| 1 | Cost type | Budget £ | Actual £ | Variance £ | Adverse (A)/ Favourable (F) |
| 2 | Income | 136,500 | 139,125 | 2,625 | F |
| 3 | Direct materials | 25,500 | 20,200 | 5,300 | F |
| 4 | Direct labour | 55,000 | 56,125 | 1,125 | A |
| 5 | Production overheads | 35,000 | 32,120 | 2,880 | F |

(b)

| | D |
|---|---|
| 1 | Variance £ |
| 2 | =(B2-C2) |
| 3 | =(B3-C3) |
| 4 | =(B4-C4) |
| 5 | =(B5-C5) |

## Task 17

(a)

| | A | B | C | D | E | F |
|---|---|---|---|---|---|---|
| 1 | Cost type | Budget £ | Variance £ | Adverse/ Favourable | Variance as percentage of budget % | Significant (S Not significar (NS) |
| 2 | Direct materials | 170,000 | 8,750 | Adverse | 5.1 | S |
| 3 | Direct labour | 140,000 | 9,025 | Adverse | 6.4 | S |
| 4 | Production overheads | 52,000 | 4,218 | Favourable | 8.1 | S |
| 5 | Administration overheads | 45,000 | 5,810 | Adverse | 12.9 | S |
| 6 | Selling and Distribution overheads | 22,000 | 500 | Adverse | 2.3 | NS |

(b)

| | E |
|---|---|
| **1** | Variance as percentage of budget % |
| **2** | =(C2/B2) |
| **3** | =(C3/B3) |
| **4** | =(C4/B4) |
| **5** | =(C5/B5) |
| **6** | =(C6/B6) |

# BPP PRACTICE ASSESSMENT 3
# BASIC COSTING

**Time allowed: 2 hours**

PRACTICE ASSESSMENT 3

# Basic Costing BPP practice assessment 3

## Task 1

(a) **Identify whether the following statements are True or False by putting a tick in the relevant column of the table below.**

|  | True | False |
|---|---|---|
| The FIFO method of inventory valuation would suit businesses with perishable goods where the oldest items are used first |  |  |
| AVCO costs issues of inventory at the oldest purchase price |  |  |
| Direct costs are generally variable |  |  |
| With variable costs, the total cost increases in proportion to the increase in output |  |  |

(b) A business receives an invoice for a batch order of paint delivered last week.

**Indicate which of the characteristics below concern the financial accounting system and which concern the management accounting system by putting a tick in the relevant column of the table below.**

| Characteristic | Financial accounting | Management accounting |
|---|---|---|
| The paint was bought on credit |  |  |
| The paint was coded to the production cost centre code |  |  |
| The paint was bought from Albion Paints |  |  |

## Task 2

(a) Asquith Ltd is a manufacturer of gloves.

**Classify the following costs by element (materials, labour or overheads) by putting a tick in the relevant column of the table below.**

| Cost | Materials | Labour | Overheads |
|---|---|---|---|
| Telephone charges for the sales office | | | |
| Glue used in making the gloves | | | |
| Oil for glove pressing machine | | | |
| Salary of the financial controller | | | |

(b) Baldwin Ltd is in business as sign painters.

**Classify the following costs by nature (direct or indirect) by putting a tick in the relevant column of the table below.**

| Cost | Direct | Indirect |
|---|---|---|
| Rent of factory premises | | |
| Varnish used on signboards | | |
| Wages of sign painters | | |
| Wages of supervisor | | |

## Task 3

(a)  Blair Ltd makes and sells waffle irons.

**Classify the following costs by function (production, administration, selling and distribution, or finance) by putting a tick in the relevant column of the table below.**

| Cost | Production | Administration | Selling and distribution | Finance |
|------|------------|----------------|--------------------------|---------|
| Interest on loan taken out to buy new machines to make the waffle irons | | | | |
| Maintenance costs for the machines to make the waffle irons | | | | |
| Wages for part-time secretary to the office manager | | | | |
| Photographic costs incurred in the most recent advertising campaign | | | | |

(b)  Brown Ltd is a manufacturer of traditional Scottish fudge.

**Classify the following costs by their behaviour (fixed, variable, or semi-variable) by putting a tick in the relevant column of the table below.**

| Cost | Fixed | Variable | Semi-variable |
|------|-------|----------|---------------|
| Packaging for the fudge tablets | | | |
| Advertising costs for the year | | | |
| Gas for the fudge kettles. This includes a standing charge | | | |
| Sugar used to make the fudge | | | |

## Task 4

Wilson Ltd makes wetsuits. It uses a numerical coding structure based on one profit centre and three cost centres as outlined below. Each code has a sub-code so each transaction will be coded as \*\*\*/\*\*\*.

| Profit/Cost centre | Code | Sub-classification | Sub-code |
|---|---|---|---|
| Sales | 100 | European sales | 100 |
| | | Asian sales | 200 |
| Production | 200 | Direct cost | 100 |
| | | Indirect cost | 200 |
| Administration | 300 | Direct cost | 100 |
| | | Indirect cost | 200 |
| Selling and Distribution | 400 | Direct cost | 100 |
| | | Indirect cost | 200 |

Code the following revenue and expense transactions using the table below.

| Transaction | Code |
|---|---|
| Glue used to seal the wetsuits | |
| Factory rates | |
| Sales to France | |
| Sales to China | |
| Salaries of sales representatives | |
| Spare parts for stitching machines | |

## Task 5

Heath Limited makes handbags and uses an alpha-numeric coding system for its elements of cost (materials, labour or overheads) and then further classifies each element by nature (direct or indirect cost) as below. So, for example, the code for direct materials is M100.

| Element of cost | Code | Nature of cost | Code |
| --- | --- | --- | --- |
| Materials | M | Direct | 100 |
| | | Indirect | 200 |
| Labour | L | Direct | 100 |
| | | Indirect | 200 |
| Overheads | O | Direct | 100 |
| | | Indirect | 200 |

**Code the following costs, extracted from invoices and payroll, using the table below.**

| Cost | Code |
| --- | --- |
| Salary of bag stitcher | |
| Monthly fees for bookkeeper to come in and write up the ledgers | |
| Thread used in stitching bags | |
| Cleaning materials used to clean the workshop | |

## Task 6

(a) **Identify the following statements as either True or False by putting a tick in the relevant column of the table below.**

| | True | False |
| --- | --- | --- |
| Fixed costs are affected in the short term by changes in production level | | |
| Variable costs are also known as period costs | | |
| If a cost is made up of a fixed charge plus a charge per unit, it is a semi-variable cost | | |

(b) **Classify the following costs for a car manufacturer as either fixed or variable by putting a tick in the relevant column of the table below.**

| Costs | Fixed | Variable |
|---|---|---|
| Oil in new cars delivered to showrooms | | |
| Wages of production line workers paid at a time-rate | | |
| Rent of paint shop | | |
| Interest on loan taken out to fund purchase of new robots | | |

## Task 7

(a) **Which ONE of the following costs is an overhead for a business which manufactures sofas?**

| | Overhead |
|---|---|
| Cost of material used to upholster sofas | |
| Cost of skilled carpenters who make the sofa frames | |
| Cost of insurance against injury to workers | |
| Cost of plastic to wrap finished sofas | |

(b) Attlee Ltd makes a single product and for a production level of 15,000 units has the following cost details:

Materials 5,000 kilos at £7 per kilo
Labour 4,000 hours at £8 an hour
Overheads £30,000

**Complete the table below to show the unit cost at the production level of 15,000 units, correct to one decimal place.**

| Element | Unit cost at 15,000 units £ |
|---|---|
| Materials | |
| Labour | |
| Overheads | |
| Total | |

# Task 8

(a) **Reorder the following headings and costs into a manufacturing account format on the right side of the table below for the year ended 31 December.**

| Heading | Cost £ | Manufacturing account | £ |
|---|---|---|---|
| Closing inventory of work in progress | 37,500 | | |
| Direct labour | 363,750 | | |
| Opening inventory of raw materials | 26,250 | | |
| Closing inventory of finished goods | 93,750 | | |
| Closing inventory of raw materials | 37,500 | | |
| Manufacturing overheads | 198,750 | | |
| COST OF GOODS SOLD | | | |
| MANUFACTURING COST | | | |
| Purchases of raw materials | 187,500 | | |
| Opening inventory of work in progress | 30,000 | | |
| Opening inventory of finished goods | 112,500 | | |
| DIRECT COST | | | |
| DIRECT MATERIALS USED | | | |
| COST OF GOODS MANUFACTURED | | | |

(b) **Enter the correct figures for the following costs which were not provided in part (a).**

| Manufacturing account | £ |
|---|---|
| DIRECT MATERIALS USED | |
| DIRECT COST | |
| MANUFACTURING COST | |
| COST OF GOODS MANUFACTURED | |
| COST OF GOODS SOLD | |

## Task 9

You are told the opening inventory of a single good for resale in the warehouse is 1,500 units at £4.00 per unit. During the month 1,700 units at £5.00 per unit are received and the following week 2,000 units are issued for sale.

(a) **Identify the valuation method described in the statements below.**

| Statement | FIFO | LIFO | AVCO |
|---|---|---|---|
| The closing inventory is valued at £6,000 | | | |
| The issue of 3,200 units is costed at £9,062 | | | |
| The closing inventory is valued at £4,800 | | | |

You are told the opening inventory of a single good for resale in the warehouse is 1,500 units at £4.00 per unit. During the month 1,700 units at £5.00 per unit are received and the following week 2,000 units are issued for sale.

(b) **Identify whether the statements in the table below are true or false by putting a tick in the relevant column.**

| Statement | True | False |
|---|---|---|
| AVCO values the closing inventory at £5,437.50 | | |
| FIFO costs the issue of 3,200 units at £8,400.00 | | |
| LIFO costs the issue of 3,200 units at £9,700.00 | | |

## Task 10

Walpole Ltd has the following movements in a certain type of inventory into and out of its stores for the month of February:

| DATE | RECEIPTS | | ISSUES | |
|------|----------|------|--------|------|
| | Units | Cost £ | Units | Cost £ |
| February 5 | 500 | 1,000 | | |
| February 8 | 750 | 1,875 | | |
| February 12 | 1,250 | 2,500 | | |
| February 18 | | | 1,950 | |
| February 25 | 1,000 | 6,000 | | |

**Complete the table below for the issue and closing inventory values.**

| Method | Cost of issue on 18 February £ | Closing inventory at 28 February £ |
|--------|-------------------------------|-----------------------------------|
| FIFO | | |
| LIFO | | |
| AVCO | | |

............................................................................................

## Task 11

(a) An employee is paid £10.00 an hour and is expected to make 30 units an hour.

Any excess production will be paid a bonus of 50p per unit.

**Identify the following statements as being true or false by putting a tick in the relevant column of the table below.**

| Statements | True | False |
|-----------|------|-------|
| During a 35 hour week the employee produces 1,100 units so does not receive a bonus | | |
| During a 38 hour week the employee produces 1,180 units and so receives a bonus of £20 | | |
| During a 40 hour week the employee produces 1,270 units and so receives total pay of £435 | | |

............................................................................................

(b)  Shaftesbury Ltd pays a time-rate of £5.85 per hour to its direct labour for a standard 35-hour week. Any of the labour force working in excess of 35 hours is paid an overtime rate of £8.20 per hour.

**Calculate the gross wage for the week for the two workers in the table below. If no overtime is paid you should enter 0 as the overtime figure for that employee.**

| Worker | Hours worked | Basic wage £ | Overtime £ | Gross wage £ |
|---|---|---|---|---|
| G Bundchen | 35 | | | |
| L Evangelista | 37 | | | |

## Task 12

Gladstone Ltd uses a piecework method to pay labour in one of its factories. The rate used is 95p per unit produced.

**Calculate the gross wage for the week for the two workers in the table below.**

| Worker | Units produced in week | Gross wage £ |
|---|---|---|
| M Mouse | 550 units | |
| W Coyote | 490 units | |

## Task 13

Disraeli Ltd uses a time-rate method with bonus to pay its direct labour in one of its factories. The time-rate used is £13.75 per hour and a worker is expected to produce five units an hour, anything over this and the worker is paid a bonus of £3.50 per unit.

**Calculate the gross wage for the week including bonus for the three workers in the table below.**

| Worker | Hours worked | Units produced | Basic wage £ | Bonus £ | Gross wage £ |
|---|---|---|---|---|---|
| D Duck | 35 | 165 | | | |
| F Flintstone | 35 | 173 | | | |
| B Rubble | 35 | 180 | | | |

## Task 14

Gimlet Ltd makes a single product and has the following production and cost data:

Variable Costs     £6 per unit
Fixed Costs        £12,000 per month

Gimlet Ltd can choose to produce 1,000, 2,000, 3,000 or 4,000 units over its next budget period. It wishes to identify its unit cost at each level of production.

The spreadsheet below has been partly formatted in order to provide expenditure information for the three months.

(a) **Complete the formatting of the spreadsheet by selecting column headings from the picklist. Complete rows 3, 4 and 5 by inserting figures in the cells.**

|   | A | B | C | D | E |
|---|---|---|---|---|---|
| 1 | Units produced | Fixed Costs £ | ▼ | ▼ | Unit cost £ |
| 2 | 1,000 | 12,000 | 6,000 | 18,000 | 18 |
| 3 |   |   |   |   |   |
| 4 |   |   |   |   |   |
| 5 |   |   |   |   |   |

**Picklist:**

Fixed Costs £
Unit cost £
Units produced
Total Costs £
Variable Costs £

......................................................................................................

(b) **Insert the formulas in the table below that you used for rows 3, 4 and 5 of column E.**

|   | E |
|---|---|
| 3 |   |
| 4 |   |
| 5 |   |

......................................................................................................

## Task 15

Listed below are four statements about spreadsheets.

**Identify the statements as being True or False by putting a tick in the relevant column of the table below.**

| Statement | True | False |
|---|---|---|
| A formula can be used in a spreadsheet to calculate an average | | |
| To total a column of figures the Autosum formula should be used | | |
| A spreadsheet can only contain a maximum of 10 worksheets | | |
| The autocorrect facility in a spreadsheet is the only checking that a spreadsheet requires | | |

## Task 16

(a) Churchill Ltd wishes to produce a spreadsheet detailing budgeted and actual results for last month and showing variances. It had the following budget:

Income £130,000

Expenditure:

Materials    £33,750

Labour £35,000

Overheads    £30,000

**Enter the above data into the spreadsheet below, calculate the amount of each variance and then determine whether it is adverse or favourable by typing F for favourable and A for adverse in the right-hand column of the table below.**

| | A | B | C | D | E |
|---|---|---|---|---|---|
| 1 | Cost type | Budget £ | Actual £ | Variance £ | Adverse (A)/ Favourable (F) |
| 2 | Income | | 121,580 | | |
| 3 | Direct materials | | 34,250 | | |
| 4 | Direct labour | | 32,125 | | |
| 5 | Production overheads | | 29,812 | | |

(b) **Insert the formulas in the table below that you used for cells 2, 3, 4 and 5 of column D of the spreadsheet.**

| | D |
|---|---|
| 1 | Variance £ |
| 2 | |
| 3 | |
| 4 | |
| 5 | |

## Task 17

The following performance report for this month has been produced for Macmillan Ltd as summarised in the spreadsheet below. Any variance in excess of 15% of budget is deemed to be significant and should be reported to the relevant manager for review and appropriate action.

(a) Calculate each variance as a percentage of the budgeted amount, correct to one decimal place. Indicate whether each variance is significant or not significant by inserting S or NS.

| | A | B | C | D | E | F |
|---|---|---|---|---|---|---|
| 1 | Cost type | Budget £ | Variance £ | Adverse/ Favourable | Variance as percentage of budget % | Significant/ Not significant |
| 2 | Direct materials | 122,000 | 19,335 | Adverse | | |
| 3 | Direct labour | 80,000 | 8,015 | Adverse | | |
| 4 | Production overheads | 64,000 | 6,208 | Favourable | | |
| 5 | Administration overheads | 55,000 | 14,980 | Adverse | | |
| 6 | Selling and Distribution overheads | 32,000 | 3,150 | Adverse | | |

(b) **Insert the formulas in the table below that you used for cells 2, 3, 4, 5 and 6 of <u>column E</u> of the spreadsheet.**

| | E |
|---|---|
| **1** | Variance as percentage of budget % |
| **2** | |
| **3** | |
| **4** | |
| **5** | |
| **6** | |

# BPP PRACTICE ASSESSMENT 3
# BASIC COSTING

# ANSWERS

# Basic Costing BPP practice assessment 3

## Task 1

(a)

|  | True | False |
|---|---|---|
| The FIFO method of inventory valuation would suit businesses with perishable goods where the oldest items are used first | ✓ | |
| AVCO costs issues of inventory at the oldest purchase price | | ✓ |
| Direct costs are generally variable | ✓ | |
| With variable costs, the total cost increases in proportion to the increase in output | ✓ | |

(b)

| Characteristic | Financial accounting | Management accounting |
|---|---|---|
| The paint was bought on credit | ✓ | |
| The paint was coded to the production cost centre code | | ✓ |
| The paint was bought from Albion Paints | ✓ | |

## Task 2

(a)

| Cost | Materials | Labour | Overheads |
|---|---|---|---|
| Telephone charges for the sales office | | | ✓ |
| Glue used in making the gloves | ✓ | | |
| Oil for glove pressing machine | | | ✓ |
| Salary of the financial controller | | | ✓ |

(b)

| Cost | Direct | Indirect |
|------|--------|----------|
| Rent of factory premises | | ✓ |
| Varnish used on signboards | ✓ | |
| Wages of sign painters | ✓ | |
| Wages of supervisor | | ✓ |

## Task 3

(a)

| Cost | Production | Administration | Selling and distribution | Fina |
|------|-----------|----------------|--------------------------|------|
| Interest on loan taken out to buy new machines to make the waffle irons | | | | ✓ |
| Maintenance costs for the machines to make the waffle irons | ✓ | | | |
| Wages for part-time secretary to the office manager | | ✓ | | |
| Photographic costs incurred in the most recent advertising campaign | | | ✓ | |

(b)

| Cost | Fixed | Variable | Semi-variable |
|------|-------|----------|---------------|
| Packaging for the fudge tablets | | ✓ | |
| Advertising costs for the year | ✓ | | |
| Gas for the fudge kettles. This includes a standing charge | | | ✓ |
| Sugar used to make the fudge | | ✓ | |

# Task 4

| Transaction | Code |
|---|---|
| Glue used to seal the wetsuits | 200/100 |
| Factory rates | 200/200 |
| Sales to France | 100/100 |
| Sales to China | 100/200 |
| Salaries of sales representatives | 400/200 |
| Spare parts for stitching machines | 200/200 |

# Task 5

| Cost | Code |
|---|---|
| Salary of bag stitcher | L100 |
| Monthly fees for bookkeeper to come in and write up the ledgers | O200 |
| Thread used in stitching bags | M100 |
| Cleaning materials used to clean the workshop | M200 |

# Task 6

(a)

| | True | False |
|---|---|---|
| Fixed costs are affected in the short term by changes in production level | | ✓ |
| Variable costs are also known as period costs | | ✓ |
| If a cost is made up of a fixed charge plus a charge per unit, it is a semi-variable cost | ✓ | |

(b)

| Costs | Fixed | Variable |
|---|---|---|
| Oil in new cars delivered to showrooms | | ✓ |
| Wages of production line workers paid at a time-rate | ✓ | |
| Rent of paint shop | ✓ | |
| Interest on loan taken out to fund purchase of new robots | ✓ | |

## Task 7

(a)

| | Overhead |
|---|---|
| Cost of material used to upholster sofas | |
| Cost of skilled carpenters who make the sofa frames | |
| Cost of insurance against injury to workers | ✓ |
| Cost of plastic to wrap finished sofas | |

(b)

| Element | Unit cost at 15,000 units £ |
|---|---|
| Materials | 2.33 |
| Labour | 2.13 |
| Overheads | 2.00 |
| Total | 6.46 |

# Task 8

## (a)   Manufacturing Account Y/e 31 December

|  | £ |
| --- | --- |
| Opening inventory of raw materials | 26,250 |
| Purchases of raw materials | 187,500 |
| Closing inventory of raw materials | 37,500 |
| DIRECT MATERIALS USED |  |
| Direct labour | 363,750 |
| DIRECT COST |  |
| Manufacturing overheads | 198,750 |
| MANUFACTURING COST |  |
| Opening inventory of work in progress | 30,000 |
| Closing inventory of work in progress | 37,500 |
| COST OF GOODS MANUFACTURED |  |
| Opening inventory of finished goods | 112,500 |
| Closing inventory of finished goods | 93,750 |
| COST OF GOODS SOLD |  |

## (b)

| Manufacturing account | £ |
| --- | --- |
| DIRECT MATERIALS USED | 176,250 |
| DIRECT COST | 540,000 |
| MANUFACTURING COST | 738,750 |
| COST OF GOODS MANUFACTURED | 731,250 |
| COST OF GOODS SOLD | 750,000 |

# Task 9

(a)

| Statement | FIFO | LIFO | AVCO |
|---|---|---|---|
| The closing inventory is valued at £6,000 | ✓ | | |
| The issue of 3,200 units is costed at £9,062.50 | | | ✓ |
| The closing inventory is valued at £4,800 | | ✓ | |

(b)

| Statement | True | False |
|---|---|---|
| AVCO values the closing inventory at £5,437.50 | ✓ | |
| FIFO costs the issue of 3,200 units at £8,400.00 | | ✓ |
| LIFO costs the issue of 3,200 units at £9,700.00 | ✓ | |

**Workings:**

| | Units | Per unit £ | Total £ | Balance £ |
|---|---|---|---|---|
| Opening inventory | 1,500 | 4.00 | 6,000 | 6,000 |
| Received | 1,700 | 5.00 | 8,500 | 14,500 |
| | 3,200 | | | |
| Issued | (2,000) | | | |
| Closing inventory | 1,200 | | | |

| | FIFO | LIFO | AVCO |
|---|---|---|---|
| Issue | (1,500 × £4) + (500 × £5) = £8,500 | (1,700 × £5) + (300 × £4) = £9,700 | 2,000 × £14,500/3,200 = £9,062.50 |
| Closing inventory | 1,200 × £5 = £6,000 | (1,200 × £4) = £4,800 | 1,200 × £14,500/3,200 = £5,437.50 |

# Task 10

| Method | Cost of issue on 18 February | Closing inventory at 28 February |
|---|---|---|
| FIFO | (1,000 + 1,875 + (700/1,250 × 2,500)) = **£4,275** | 6,000 + (550/1,250 × 2,500) = **£7,100** |
| LIFO | (2,500 + (700/750 × 1,875)) = **£4,250** | (6,000 + 1,000 + (50/750 × 1,875)) = **£7,125** |
| AVCO | 1,950/2,500 × 5,375 = **£4,192.50** | (550/2,500 × 5,375) + 6,000 = **£7,182.50** |

# Task 11 (9 marks)

(a)

| Statements | True | False |
|---|---|---|
| During a 35 hour week the employee produces 1,100 units so does not receive a bonus | | ✓ |
| During a 38 hour week the employee produces 1,180 units and so receives a bonus of £20 | ✓ | |
| During a 40 hour week the employee produces 1,270 units and so receives total pay of £435 | ✓ | |

**Workings**

1  Expected output: 35 × 30 = 1,050 units. With a 50 unit excess the employee should receive a bonus (of £25)

2  Expected output: 38 × 30 = 1,140 units. Excess: 40 × £0.50 = £20

3  Expected output: 40 x 30 = 1,200 units. Excess: 70 × £0.50 = £35.
   Total pay: (40 × £10) + £35 = £435

(b)

| Worker | Hours worked | Basic wage £ | Overtime £ | Gross wage £ |
|---|---|---|---|---|
| G Bundchen | 35 | 204.75 | 0 | 204.75 |
| L Evangelista | 37 | 204.75 | 16.40 | 221.15 |

## Task 12

| Worker | Units produced in week | Gross wage £ |
|---|---|---|
| M Mouse | 550 units | 522.50 |
| W Coyote | 490 units | 465.50 |

## Task 13

| Worker | Hours worked | Units produced | Basic wage £ | Bonus £ | Gross wage £ |
|---|---|---|---|---|---|
| D Duck | 35 | 165 | 481.25 | 0 | 481.25 |
| F Flintstone | 35 | 173 | 481.25 | 0 | 481.25 |
| B Rubble | 35 | 180 | 481.25 | 17.50 | 498.75 |

## Task 14

(a)

| | A | B | C | D | E |
|---|---|---|---|---|---|
| 1 | Units produced | Fixed Costs £ | Variable Costs £ | Total Costs £ | Unit cost £ |
| 2 | 1,000 | 12,000 | 6,000 | 18,000 | 18 |
| 3 | 2,000 | 12,000 | 12,000 | 24,000 | 12 |
| 4 | 3,000 | 12,000 | 18,000 | 30,000 | 10 |
| 5 | 4,000 | 12,000 | 24,000 | 36,000 | 9 |

(b)

| | E |
|---|---|
| 3 | =(D3/A3) |
| 4 | =(D4/A4) |
| 5 | =(D5/A5) |

# Task 15

| Statement | True | False |
|---|---|---|
| A formula can be used in a spreadsheet to calculate an average | ✓ | |
| To total a column of figures the Autosum formula should be used | ✓ | |
| A spreadsheet can only contain a maximum of 10 worksheets | | ✓ |
| The autocorrect facility in a spreadsheet is the only checking that a spreadsheet requires | | ✓ |

# Task 16

(a)

| | A | B | C | D | E |
|---|---|---|---|---|---|
| 1 | Cost type | Budget £ | Actual £ | Variance £ | Adverse (A)/ Favourable (F) |
| 2 | Income | 130,000 | 121,580 | 8,420 | A |
| 3 | Direct materials | 33,750 | 34,250 | 500 | A |
| 4 | Direct labour | 35,000 | 32,125 | 2,875 | F |
| 5 | Production overheads | 30,000 | 29,812 | 188 | F |

(b)

| | D |
|---|---|
| 1 | Variance £ |
| 2 | =(B2-C2) |
| 3 | =(B3-C3) |
| 4 | =(B4-C4) |
| 5 | =(B5-C5) |

## Task 17

(a)

| | A | B | C | D | E | F |
|---|---|---|---|---|---|---|
| 1 | Cost type | Budget £ | Variance £ | Adverse/ Favourable | Variance as percentage of budget % | Significant/ Not significant |
| 2 | Direct materials | 122,000 | 19,335 | Adverse | 15.8 | S |
| 3 | Direct labour | 80,000 | 8,015 | Adverse | 10.0 | NS |
| 4 | Production overheads | 64,000 | 6,208 | Favourable | 9.7 | NS |
| 5 | Administration overheads | 55,000 | 14,980 | Adverse | 27.2 | S |
| 6 | Selling and Distribution overheads | 32,000 | 3,150 | Adverse | 9.8 | NS |

(b)

| | E |
|---|---|
| 1 | Variance as percentage of budget % |
| 2 | =(C2/B2) |
| 3 | =(C3/B3) |
| 4 | =(C4/B4) |
| 5 | =(C5/B5) |
| 6 | =(C6/B6) |

# BPP PRACTICE ASSESSMENT 4
# BASIC COSTING

**Time allowed: 2 hours**

PRACTICE ASSESSMENT 4

# Basic Costing BPP practice assessment 4

## Task 1

(a) **Identify the following statements about a manufacturing business as True or False by putting a tick in the relevant column of the table below.**

| | True | False |
|---|---|---|
| Variable cost per unit remains constant over the level of activity | | |
| Overheads always remain constant over any range of activity | | |
| Finished goods inventory is kept until transferred to the production line | | |
| A time-rate system of pay is based on hours worked and pay per hour | | |
| A favourable variance means budgeted sales are greater than actual sales | | |

(b) Management are constantly making decisions about how the business operates. These are short-term, medium-term or long-term decisions. The table below lists an example of each type.

**Match the example to the correct decision by putting a tick in the relevant column of the table below.**

| Characteristic | Short-term | Medium-term | Long-term |
|---|---|---|---|
| Where to locate a factory | | | |
| Whether to work overtime in the factory | | | |
| Whether to take out a further loan to finance the business | | | |

## Task 2

(a) Clifton Ltd makes glass bottles.

**Classify the following costs by element (materials, labour or overheads) by putting a tick in the relevant column of the table below.**

| Cost | Materials | Labour | Overhead |
|---|---|---|---|
| Spare parts for the glass firing kiln | | | |
| Rent on the workshop | | | |
| Salaries of glass blowers | | | |
| Sand used in making the bottles | | | |

(b) Easton Ltd operates as a petrol station.

**Classify the following costs by nature (direct or indirect) by putting a tick in the relevant column of the table below.**

| Cost | Direct | Indirect |
|---|---|---|
| Petrol in the pumps | | |
| Business rates for the petrol station | | |
| Wages of pump attendants | | |
| Salary of forecourt supervisor for the petrol company | | |

## Task 3

(a) St Paul Ltd makes guitars.

**Classify the following costs by function (production, administration, selling and distribution or finance) by putting a tick in the relevant column of the table below.**

| Cost | Production | Administration | Selling and Distribution | Finance |
|---|---|---|---|---|
| Purchase of balsa wood for making guitars | | | | |
| Advertising the instruments in *Music Weekly* | | | | |
| Secretarial wages | | | | |
| Salaries of craftspeople making the instruments | | | | |

(b) Highbridge Ltd is a manufacturer of children's toys.

**Classify the following costs by their behaviour (fixed, variable, or semi-variable) by putting a tick in the relevant column of the table below.**

| Cost | Fixed | Variable | Semi-variable |
|---|---|---|---|
| Felt used in making the toys | | | |
| Marketing costs for the year | | | |
| Telephone charges for the office that include a fixed line rental and call charges | | | |
| Electricity charges for the sewing machines that include a basic charge and a unit consumption charge | | | |

## Task 4

Burnham Ltd makes bicycles. It uses a numerical coding structure based on one profit centre and three cost centres as outlined below. Each code has a sub-code so each transaction will be coded as */***.

| Profit/Cost centre | Code | Sub-classification | Sub-code |
|---|---|---|---|
| Sales | 9 | Children's bike sales | 100 |
| | | Adult bike sales | 200 |
| Production | 8 | Direct cost | 100 |
| | | Indirect cost | 200 |
| Administration | 7 | Direct cost | 100 |
| | | Indirect cost | 200 |
| Selling and Distribution | 6 | Direct cost | 100 |
| | | Indirect cost | 200 |

**Code the following income and expense transactions using the table below.**

| Transaction | Code |
|---|---|
| Electricity charge for the upstairs offices | |
| Petrol for warehouse van | |
| Sales of adult bikes | |
| Sales of children's bikes | |
| Enamel paint for bicycles | |
| Factory supervisor wages | |

## Task 5

Weston Limited operates a convenience store and uses an alpha-numeric coding system for its elements of cost (materials, labour or overheads) and then further classifies each element by nature (direct or indirect cost) as below. Each code has a sub-code so each transaction will be coded as **/***.

| Element of cost | Code | Nature of cost | Code |
|---|---|---|---|
| Materials | MA | Direct | 100 |
| | | Indirect | 200 |
| Labour | LA | Direct | 100 |
| | | Indirect | 200 |
| Overheads | OV | Direct | 100 |
| | | Indirect | 200 |

**Code the following costs using the table below.**

| Cost | Code |
|---|---|
| Wages of shop staff | |
| Fees for bookkeeper | |
| Wholesale cost of newspapers | |
| Cleaning materials used by shop cleaner | |
| Rent and rates on the shop premises | |

## Task 6

(a) **Identify the following statements as either True or False by putting a tick in the relevant column of the table below.**

|  | True | False |
|---|---|---|
| Fixed costs are not affected in the short term by changes in production level |  |  |
| Variable costs are often known as period costs |  |  |
| Semi-variable costs are fixed over a certain range of activity |  |  |

(b) **Classify the following costs for a boat manufacturer as either fixed or variable by putting a tick in the relevant column of the table below.**

| Costs | Fixed | Variable |
|---|---|---|
| Steel used in making boat hull |  |  |
| Wages of workers on the assembly line paid piece-rate |  |  |
| Salaries of managers |  |  |
| Rent for offices used by sales staff |  |  |

## Task 7

(a) Taunton Ltd is costing a single product, which has the following cost details:

Variable costs per unit

| Materials | £6.50 |
| Labour | £8.50 |
| Total fixed costs | £150,000 |

**Complete the following total cost and unit cost table for a production level of 10,000 units.**

| Element | Total cost £ | Unit cost at 10,000 units £ |
|---|---|---|
| Materials | | |
| Labour | | |
| Overheads | | |
| Total | | |

(b) Kingswear Ltd makes a single product and for a production level of 30,000 units has the following cost details:

| Materials 6,000 kilos at | £15 per kilo |
| Labour 5,000 hours at | £12 an hour |
| Overheads | £50,000 |

**Complete the table below to show the unit cost at the production level of 30,000 units.**

| Element | Unit cost at 30,000 units £ |
|---|---|
| Materials | |
| Labour | |
| Overheads | |
| Total | |

## Task 8

(a) **Reorder the following headings and costs into a manufacturing account format on the right side of the table below for the year ended 31 January.**

| Heading | Cost £ | Manufacturing account | £ |
|---|---|---|---|
| Closing inventory of work in progress | 27,150 | | |
| Direct labour | 244,150 | | |
| Opening inventory of raw materials | 19,150 | | |
| Closing inventory of finished goods | 64,150 | | |
| Closing inventory of raw materials | 27,150 | | |
| Manufacturing overheads | 134,150 | | |
| COST OF GOODS SOLD | | | |
| MANUFACTURING COST | | | |
| Purchases of raw materials | 127,150 | | |
| Opening inventory of work in progress | 22,150 | | |
| Opening inventory of finished goods | 77,150 | | |
| DIRECT COST | | | |
| DIRECT MATERIALS USED | | | |
| COST OF GOODS MANUFACTURED | | | |

(b) **Enter the correct figures for the following costs which were not provided in part (a).**

| Manufacturing account | £ |
|---|---|
| DIRECT MATERIALS USED | |
| DIRECT COST | |
| MANUFACTURING COST | |
| COST OF GOODS MANUFACTURED | |
| COST OF GOODS SOLD | |

## Task 9

You are told the opening inventory of a single good for resale in the warehouse is 1,700 units at £3.00 per unit. During the month 2,500 units at £4.00 per unit are received and the following week 1,900 units are issued for sale.

(a) **Identify the valuation method described in the statements below.**

| Statement | FIFO | LIFO | AVCO |
|---|---|---|---|
| The closing inventory is valued at £8,269 | | | |
| The issue of 1,900 units is costed at £5,900 | | | |
| The closing inventory is valued at £7,500 | | | |

You are told the opening inventory of a single good for resale in the warehouse is 1,700 units at £3.00 per unit. During the month 2,500 units at £4.00 per unit are received and the following week 1,900 units are issued for sale.

(b) **Identify whether the statements in the table below are true or false by putting a tick in the relevant column.**

| Statement | True | False |
|---|---|---|
| FIFO values the closing inventory at £9,200 | | |
| LIFO costs the issue of 1,900 units at £7,300 | | |
| AVCO costs the issue of 1,900 units at £6,731 | | |

## Task 10

Wellington Ltd has the following movements in a certain type of inventory into and out of its stores for the month of April:

| DATE | RECEIPTS | | | ISSUES | |
|---|---|---|---|---|---|
| | Units | Cost £ | | Units | Cost £ |
| April 10 | 300 | 1,200 | | | |
| April 11 | 450 | 2,250 | | | |
| April 12 | 1,250 | 6,250 | | | |
| April 19 | | | | 1,500 | |
| April 27 | 700 | 4,900 | | | |

**Complete the table below for the issue and closing inventory values.**

| Method | Cost of issue on 19 April £ | Closing inventory at 30 April £ |
|---|---|---|
| FIFO | | |
| LIFO | | |
| AVCO | | |

## Task 11

(a) An employee is paid £7.50 an hour and is expected to make 20 units an hour.

Any excess production will be paid a bonus of £1 per unit.

**Identify the following statements as being true or false by putting a tick in the relevant column of the table below.**

| Statements | True | False |
|---|---|---|
| During a 36 hour week the employee produces 710 units so does not receive a bonus | | |
| During a 39 hour week the employee produces 815 units and so receives a bonus of £25 | | |
| During a 42 hour week the employee produces 895 units and so receives total pay of £370 | | |

(b) Park Street Ltd pays a time-rate of £9.75 per hour to its direct labour for a standard 35-hour week. Any of the labour force working in excess of 35 hours is paid an overtime rate of £12.50 per hour.

**Calculate the gross wage for the week for the two workers in the table below.**

| Worker | Hours worked | Basic wage £ | Overtime £ | Gross wage £ |
|---|---|---|---|---|
| L Hornby | 35 hours | | | |
| J Shrimpton | 42 hours | | | |

## Task 12

(a) Burnham Ltd uses a piecework method to pay labour in one of its factories. The rate used is 75p per unit produced.

**Calculate the gross wage for the week for the two workers in the table below.**

| Worker | Units produced in week | Gross wage £ |
|---|---|---|
| N Campbell | 375 units | |
| K Moss | 390 units | |

(b) **Which ONE of the following statements is an advantage of payment by the piecework method?**

| Statement | Advantage of piecework |
|---|---|
| Quality is a priority as pay is the same no matter how much is produced | |
| Employees have an incentive to produce more | |
| The method can easily be used for all direct labour employees | |

## Task 13

Bristol Ltd uses a time-rate method with bonus to pay its direct labour in one of its factories. The time-rate used is £10.50 per hour and a worker is expected to produce six units an hour, anything over this and the worker is paid a bonus of £1.50 per unit.

**Calculate the gross wage for the week including bonus for the three workers in the table below.**

| Worker | Hours worked | Units produced | Basic wage £ | Bonus £ | Gross wage £ |
|--------|--------------|----------------|--------------|---------|--------------|
| A Einstein | 35 | 160 | | | |
| N Bohr | 35 | 175 | | | |
| E Fermi | 35 | 220 | | | |

## Task 14

Millman Ltd makes a single product and has the following income and expenditure data:

Sales revenue     £27 per unit

Variable costs     £15 per unit

Fixed costs     £25,000 per month

The number of units sold by Millman Ltd in the last three months is as follows:

June        2,000 units

July        2,100 units

August     2,300 units

The spreadsheet below has been partly formatted in order to provide income and expenditure information for the three months.

(a) **Complete the formatting of the spreadsheet by selecting column headings from the picklist. Insert figures in the cells for July, August and Total.**

| | A | B | C | D | E | F |
|---|---|---|---|---|---|---|
| 1 | | Variable cost £ | ▼ | ▼ | Sales revenue £ | ▼ |
| 2 | June | 30,000 | 25,000 | 55,000 | 54,000 | -1,000 |
| 3 | July | | | | | |
| 4 | August | | | | | |
| 5 | Total | | | | | |

**Picklist:**

Total cost £
Variable cost £
Profit/(loss) £
Sales revenue £
Fixed cost £

---

(b) **Insert the formulas in the table below that you need for cells B5, C5, D5 and F5.**

|   | A | B | C | D | E | F |
|---|---|---|---|---|---|---|
| 5 |   |   |   |   |   |   |

---

## Task 15

Listed below are four statements about spreadsheets.

**Identify the statements as being True or False by putting a tick in the relevant column of the table below.**

| Statement | True | False |
|---|---|---|
| A formula in a spreadsheet must always start with an = sign | | |
| Sorting the data in a spreadsheet can be achieved by clicking on the ascending order button | | |
| A worksheet can only contain a maximum of 100 columns and 100 rows | | |
| The formula for calculating an average in a spreadsheet =AVERAGE(B2:B5) calculates the arithmetic mean | | |

---

## Task 16

(a) Wills Ltd has produced a spreadsheet detailing budgeted costs for last month. Actual results were as follows:

| | |
|---|---|
| Direct materials | 10,000 kgs at £26.20 per kg |
| Direct labour | £73,125 |
| Production overheads | £15,120 |
| Administration overheads | £21,950 |
| Selling and Distribution overheads | £24,950 |

Enter the above data into the spreadsheet below, calculate the amount of each variance and then determine whether it is adverse or favourable by typing F for favourable and A for adverse in the right-hand column of the table below.

| | A | B | C | D | E |
|---|---|---|---|---|---|
| | Cost type | Budget £ | Actual £ | Variance £ | Adverse/Favourable |
| 1 | | | | | |
| 2 | Direct materials | 25,500 | | | |
| 3 | Direct labour | 57,000 | | | |
| 4 | Production overheads | 18,000 | | | |
| 5 | Administration overheads | 22,000 | | | |
| 6 | Selling and Distribution overheads | 23,000 | | | |

(b) Insert the formula in the table below that you used for cells C2 and D3 of the spreadsheet.

| | C | D |
|---|---|---|
| 1 | Actual £ | Variance £ |
| 2 | | |
| 3 | | |

## Task 17

(a) The following performance report for this month has been produced for Tiverton Ltd as summarised in the spreadsheet below. Any variance in excess of 10% of budget is deemed to be significant and should be reported to the relevant manager for review and appropriate action.

**Calculate each variance as a percentage of the budgeted amount, correct to one decimal place. Indicate whether each variance is significant or not significant by inserting S or NS.**

| | A | B | C | D | E | F |
|---|---|---|---|---|---|---|
| 1 | Cost type | Budget £ | Variance £ | Adverse/ Favourable | Variance as percentage of budget % | Significant/ Not significant |
| 2 | Income | 220,000 | 5,450 | Adverse | | |
| 3 | Direct materials | 125,000 | 12,335 | Favourable | | |
| 4 | Direct labour | 20,000 | 4,010 | Adverse | | |
| 5 | Production overheads | 45,000 | 4,208 | Favourable | | |

.................................................................................................

(b) **Insert the formulas in the table below that you used for cells 2, 3, 4 and 5 of <u>column E</u> of the spreadsheet.**

| | E |
|---|---|
| 1 | Variance as percentage of budget % |
| 2 | |
| 3 | |
| 4 | |
| 5 | |

.................................................................................................

# BPP PRACTICE ASSESSMENT 4
# BASIC COSTING

# ANSWERS

# Basic Costing BPP practice assessment 4

## Task 1

(a)

|  | True | False |
|---|:---:|:---:|
| Variable cost per unit remains constant over the level of activity | ✓ | |
| Overheads always remain constant over any range of activity | | ✓ |
| Finished goods inventory is kept until transferred to the production line | ✓ | |
| A time-rate system of pay is based on hours worked and pay per hour | ✓ | |
| A favourable variance means budgeted sales are greater than actual sales | | ✓ |

(b)

| Characteristic | Short-term | Medium-term | Long-term |
|---|:---:|:---:|:---:|
| Where to locate a factory | | | ✓ |
| Whether to work overtime in the factory | ✓ | | |
| Whether to take out a further loan to finance the business | | ✓ | |

## Task 2

(a)

| Cost | Materials | Labour | Overheads |
|---|:---:|:---:|:---:|
| Spare parts for the glass firing kiln | ✓ | | |
| Rent on the workshop | | | ✓ |
| Salaries of glass blowers | | ✓ | |
| Sand used in making the bottles | ✓ | | |

(b)

| Cost | Direct | Indirect |
|---|---|---|
| Petrol in the pumps | ✓ | |
| Business rates for the petrol station | | ✓ |
| Wages of pump attendants | ✓ | |
| Salary of forecourt supervisor for the petrol company | | ✓ |

## Task 3

(a)

| Cost | Production | Administration | Selling and Distribution | Financ |
|---|---|---|---|---|
| Purchase of balsa wood for making guitars | ✓ | | | |
| Advertising the instruments in *Music Weekly* | | | ✓ | |
| Secretarial wages | | ✓ | | |
| Salaries of craftspeople making the instruments | ✓ | | | |

(b)

| Cost | Fixed | Variable | Semi-variable |
|---|---|---|---|
| Felt used in making the toys | | ✓ | |
| Marketing costs for the year | ✓ | | |
| Telephone charges for the office that include a fixed line rental and call charges | | | ✓ |
| Electricity charges for the sewing machines that include a basic charge and a unit consumption charge | | | ✓ |

# Task 4

| Transaction | Code |
|---|---|
| Electricity charge for the upstairs offices | 7/200 |
| Petrol for warehouse van | 6/200 |
| Sales of adult bikes | 9/200 |
| Sales of children's bikes | 9/100 |
| Enamel paint for bicycles | 8/100 |
| Factory supervisor wages | 8/200 |

# Task 5

| Cost | Code |
|---|---|
| Wages of shop staff | LA100 |
| Fees for bookkeeper | OV200 |
| Wholesale cost of newspapers | MA100 |
| Cleaning materials used by shop cleaner | MA200 |
| Rent and rates on the shop premises | OV200 |

# Task 6

(a)

| | True | False |
|---|---|---|
| Fixed costs are not affected in the short term by changes in production level | ✓ | |
| Variable costs are often known as period costs | | ✓ |
| Semi-variable costs are fixed over a certain range of activity | | ✓ |

(b)

| Costs | Fixed | Variable |
|---|---|---|
| Steel used in making boat hull | | ✓ |
| Wages of workers on the assembly line paid piece-rate | | ✓ |
| Salaries of managers | ✓ | |
| Rent for offices used by sales staff | ✓ | |

## Task 7

(a)

| Element | Total cost £ | Unit cost at 10,000 units £ |
|---|---|---|
| Materials | 65,000 | 6.50 |
| Labour | 85,000 | 8.50 |
| Overheads | 150,000 | 15.00 |
| Total | 300,000 | 30.00 |

(b)

| Element | Unit cost at 30,000 units £ |
|---|---|
| Materials | 3.00 |
| Labour | 2.00 |
| Overheads | 1.67 |
| Total | 6.67 |

# Task 8

(a) **Manufacturing Account      Y/e 31 January**

|  | £ |
|---|---|
| Opening inventory of raw materials | 19,150 |
| Purchases of raw materials | 127,150 |
| Closing inventory of raw materials | 27,150 |
| DIRECT MATERIALS USED |  |
| Direct labour | 244,150 |
| DIRECT COST |  |
| Manufacturing overheads | 134,150 |
| MANUFACTURING COST |  |
| Opening inventory of work in progress | 22,150 |
| Closing inventory of work in progress | 27,150 |
| COST OF GOODS MANUFACTURED |  |
| Opening inventory of finished goods | 77,150 |
| Closing inventory of finished goods | 64,150 |
| COST OF GOODS SOLD |  |

(b)

| Manufacturing account | £ |
|---|---|
| DIRECT MATERIALS USED | 119,150 |
| DIRECT COST | 363,300 |
| MANUFACTURING COST | 497,450 |
| COST OF GOODS MANUFACTURED | 492,450 |
| COST OF GOODS SOLD | 505,450 |

## Task 9

### (a)

| Statement | FIFO | LIFO | AVCO |
|---|---|---|---|
| The closing inventory is valued at £8,269 | | | ✓ |
| The issue of 1,900 units is costed at £5,900 | ✓ | | |
| The closing inventory is valued at £7,500 | | ✓ | |

### (b)

| Statement | True | False |
|---|---|---|
| FIFO values the closing inventory at £9,200 | ✓ | |
| LIFO costs the issue of 1,900 units at £7,300 | | ✓ |
| AVCO costs the issue of 1,900 units at £6,731 | | ✓ |

**Workings:**

| | Units | Per unit £ | Total £ | Balance £ |
|---|---|---|---|---|
| Opening inventory | 1,700 | 3 | 5,100 | 5,100 |
| Received | 2,500 | 4 | 10,000 | 15,100 |
| | 4,200 | | | |
| Issued | (1,900) | | | |
| Closing inventory | 2,300 | | | |

| | FIFO | LIFO | AVCO |
|---|---|---|---|
| Issue | $(1,700 \times £3) + (200 \times £4) = £5,900$ | $1,900 \times £4 = £7,600$ | $1,900 \times £15,100/4,200 = £6,831$ |
| Closing inventory | $2,300 \times £4 = £9,200$ | $(1,700 \times £3) + (600 \times £4) = £7,500$ | $2,300 \times £15,100/4,200 = £8,269$ |

# Task 10

| Method | Cost of issue on 19 April £ | Closing inventory at 30 April £ |
|--------|------------------------------|----------------------------------|
| FIFO | (1,200 + 2,250 + (750/1,250 × 6,250)) = **£7,200** | (4,900 + (500/1,250 × 6,250)) = **£7,400** |
| LIFO | (6,250 + (250/450 × 2,250)) = **£7,500** | (4,900 + 1,200 + (200/450 × 2,250)) = **£7,100** |
| AVCO | 1,500/2,000 × 9,700 = **£7,275** | (4,900 + (500/2,000 × 9,700)) = **£7,325** |

# Task 11

(a)

| Statements | True | False |
|------------|------|-------|
| During a 36 hour week the employee produces 710 units so does not receive a bonus | ✓ | |
| During a 39 hour week the employee produces 815 units and so receives a bonus of £25 | | ✓ |
| During a 42 hour week the employee produces 895 units and so receives total pay of £370 | ✓ | |

**Workings**

1     Expected output: 36 × 20 = 720 units. With a 10 unit shortfall the employee will not receive a bonus

2     Expected output: 39 × 20 = 780 units. Excess: 35 × £1 = £35

3     Expected output: 42 × 20 = 840 units. Excess: 55 × £1 = £55. Total pay: (42 × £7.50) + £55 = £370

(b)

| Worker | Hours worked | Basic wage £ | Overtime £ | Gross wage £ |
|--------|--------------|--------------|------------|--------------|
| L Hornby | 35 hours | 341.25 | 0 | 341.25 |
| J Shrimpton | 42 hours | 341.25 | 87.50 | 428.75 |

# Task 12

(a)

| Worker | Units produced in week | Gross wage £ |
|---|---|---|
| N Campbell | 375 units | 281.25 |
| K Moss | 390 units | 292.50 |

(b)

| Statement | Advantage of piecework |
|---|---|
| Quality is a priority as pay is the same no matter how much is produced | |
| This method gives employees an incentive to produce more | ✓ |
| Can be used for all direct labour employees | |

# Task 13

| Worker | Hours worked | Units produced | Basic wage £ | Bonus £ | Gross wage £ |
|---|---|---|---|---|---|
| A Einstein | 35 | 160 | 367.50 | 0 | 367.50 |
| N Bohr | 35 | 175 | 367.50 | 0 | 367.50 |
| E Fermi | 35 | 220 | 367.50 | 15 | 382.50 |

# Task 14

(a)

|   | A | B | C | D | E | F |
|---|---|---|---|---|---|---|
| 1 |   | Variable cost £ | Fixed cost £ | Total costs £ | Sales revenue £ | Profit/(loss) £ |
| 2 | June | 30,000 | 25,000 | 55,000 | 54,000 | (1,000) |
| 3 | July | 31,500 | 25,000 | 56,500 | 56,700 | 200 |
| 4 | August | 34,500 | 25,000 | 59,500 | 62,100 | 2,600 |
| 5 | Total | 96,000 | 75,000 | 171,000 | 172,800 | 1,800 |

(b)

|   | A | B | C | D | E | F |
|---|---|---|---|---|---|---|
| 5 |   | =SUM(B2:B4) or =(B2+B3+B4) | =SUM(C2:C4) or =(C2+C3+C4) | =SUM(D2:D4) or =(D2+D3+D4) Or =(B5+C5) |   | =SUM(F2:F4) or =(F2+F3+F4) Or =(E5-D5) |

# Task 15

| Statement | True | False |
|---|---|---|
| A formula in a spreadsheet must always start with an = sign | ✓ |   |
| Sorting the data in a spreadsheet can be achieved by clicking on the ascending order button | ✓ |   |
| A worksheet can only contain a maximum of 100 columns and 100 rows |   | ✓ |
| The formula for calculating an average in a spreadsheet =AVERAGE(B2:B5) calculates the arithmetic mean | ✓ |   |

# Task 16

(a)

| | A | B | C | D | E |
|---|---|---|---|---|---|
| 1 | Cost type | Budget £ | Actual £ | Variance £ | Adverse/ Favourable |
| 2 | Direct materials | 25,500 | 26,200 | 700 | A |
| 3 | Direct labour | 57,000 | 73,125 | 16,125 | A |
| 4 | Production overheads | 18,000 | 15,120 | 2,880 | F |
| 5 | Administration overheads | 22,000 | 21,950 | 50 | F |
| 6 | Selling and Distribution overheads | 23,000 | 24,950 | 1,950 | A |

(b)

| | C | D |
|---|---|---|
| 1 | Actual £ | Variance £ |
| 2 | =(10000*26.2) | |
| 3 | | =(B3-C3) |

# Task 17

(a)

| | A | B | C | D | E | F |
|---|---|---|---|---|---|---|
| 1 | Cost type | Budget £ | Variance £ | Adverse/ Favourable | Variance as percentage of budget % | Significant/ Not significant |
| 2 | Income | 220,000 | 5,450 | Adverse | 2.5 | NS |
| 3 | Direct materials | 125,000 | 12,335 | Favourable | 9.9 | NS |
| 4 | Direct labour | 20,000 | 4,010 | Adverse | 20.0 | S |
| 5 | Production overheads | 45,000 | 4,208 | Favourable | 9.3 | NS |

(b)

| | E |
|---|---|
| 1 | Variance as percentage of budget % |
| 2 | =(C2/B2) |
| 3 | =(C3/B3) |
| 4 | =(C4/B4) |
| 5 | =(C5/B5) |

# BPP PRACTICE ASSESSMENT 5
# BASIC COSTING

**Time allowed: 2 hours**

# Basic Costing BPP practice assessment 5

## Task 1

(a) **Identify the following statements as True or False by putting a tick in the relevant column of the table below.**

|  | True | False |
|---|---|---|
| Fixed cost per unit rises as output in units rises |  |  |
| Variable cost per unit remains constant whatever the level of output |  |  |
| A business with an investment centre can code assets and liabilities for it |  |  |
| Many fixed costs are only fixed over a certain range of output |  |  |

(b) There are three main types of business covered in the Basic Costing unit.

**Look at the descriptions in the table below and match them to the type of business.**

| Description | Sole trader | Partnership | Limited company |
|---|---|---|---|
| A group of individuals who trade together intending to make a profit |  |  |  |
| Shareholders own the business but it is managed by directors and managers |  |  |  |
| The owner trades under their own name |  |  |  |

## Task 2

(a) Hayes Ltd makes wind chimes.

**Classify the following costs by element (materials, labour or overheads) by putting a tick in the relevant column of the table below.**

| Cost | Materials | Labour | Overheads |
|---|---|---|---|
| Wages of machine operators making the chimes | | | |
| Telephone charges for workshop floor telephone | | | |
| Tin used in making the chimes | | | |
| Salary of the supervisor on the workshop floor | | | |

(b) Elmer Ltd is in business as a tailor of men's clothing.

**Classify the following costs by nature (direct or indirect) by putting a tick in the relevant column of the table below.**

| Cost | Direct | Indirect |
|---|---|---|
| Buttons used on suit jackets | | |
| Rent and rates for shop and workshop | | |
| Licences paid to designers each time a suit pattern is used | | |
| Oil for sewing machines | | |

## Task 3

(a) Clockhouse Ltd makes clocks.

**Classify the following costs by function (production, administration, or financing) by putting a tick in the relevant column of the table below.**

| Cost | Production | Administration | Financing |
|---|---|---|---|
| Cogs used in timing movements | | | |
| Wages of payroll staff | | | |
| Overdraft charges | | | |
| Salaries of clockmakers | | | |

(b) West Wickham Ltd is a manufacturer of fibreglass panels.

**Classify the following costs by their behaviour (fixed, variable, or semi-variable) by putting a tick in the relevant column of the table below.**

| Cost | Fixed | Variable | Semi-variable |
|---|---|---|---|
| Spun fibre used in making the panels | | | |
| Salary of supervisor on the factory floor | | | |
| Electricity costs for the machines that include a standing charge | | | |
| Labour costs paid on a piecework basis | | | |

## Task 4

Catford Ltd makes toys for cats. It uses a numerical coding structure based on one profit centre and three cost centres as outlined below. Each code has a sub-code so each transaction will be coded as **/***.

| Profit/Cost centre | Code | Sub-classification | Sub-code |
|---|---|---|---|
| Sales | 01 | UK sales | 100 |
| | | Overseas sales | 200 |
| Production | 03 | Direct cost | 100 |
| | | Indirect cost | 200 |
| Administration | 05 | Direct cost | 100 |
| | | Indirect cost | 200 |
| Selling and Distribution | 07 | Direct cost | 100 |
| | | Indirect cost | 200 |

**Code the following income and expense transactions using the table below.**

| Transaction | Code |
|---|---|
| Telephone charges for the payroll department | |
| Factory rates | |
| Sales to Japan | |
| Sales to Greater Manchester | |
| Material for toys | |
| Petrol for sales vans | |

## Task 5

Ladywell Limited operates a day spa and uses an alpha-numeric coding system for its elements of cost (materials, labour or overheads) and then further classifies each element by nature (direct or indirect cost) as below. So, for example, the code for direct materials is A100.

| Element of cost | Code | Nature of cost | Code |
|---|---|---|---|
| Materials | A | Direct | 100 |
| | | Indirect | 200 |
| Labour | B | Direct | 100 |
| | | Indirect | 200 |
| Overheads | C | Direct | 100 |
| | | Indirect | 200 |

**Code the following costs using the table below.**

| Cost | Code |
|---|---|
| Wages of spa therapists | |
| Fees for designer creating new website for spa | |
| Spa salts and minerals used in treatments | |
| Cleaning materials used by cleaners at the spa | |
| Maintenance staff wages | |

## Task 6

(a) **Identify the type of cost behaviour (fixed, variable or semi-variable) described in each statement by putting a tick in the relevant column of the table below.**

| Statement | Fixed | Variable | Semi-variable |
|---|---|---|---|
| Costs of £72,000 are made up of a fixed charge of £23,000 and a further cost of £0.70 per unit at 70,000 units | | | |
| Costs of £1.80 per unit at 5,300 units and £1.06 per unit at 9,000 units | | | |
| Costs are £25,000 units at 10,000 units and £40,000 at 16,000 units | | | |

(b) **Classify the following costs as either fixed or variable by putting a tick in the relevant column of the table below.**

| Costs | Fixed | Variable |
|---|---|---|
| Cost of ink used in a printing press | | |
| Straight-line depreciation on plant and machinery | | |
| Salary of supervisor | | |
| Timber for making chairs in furniture factory | | |

## Task 7

(a) Lewisham Ltd is costing a single product, which has the following cost details:

Variable costs per unit
| | |
|---|---|
| Materials | £7.50 |
| Labour | £5.50 |

| | |
|---|---|
| Total overheads | £130,000 |

**Complete the following total cost and unit cost table for a production level of 13,000 units.**

| Element | Total cost at 13,000 units £ | Unit cost at 13,000 units £ |
|---|---|---|
| Materials | | |
| Labour | | |
| Overheads | | |
| Total | | |

(b) Christobel Ltd makes a single product and for a production level of 150,000 units has the following cost details:

| | |
|---|---|
| Materials 15,000 kilos at | £10 per kilo |
| Labour 7,500 hours at | £15 an hour |
| Overheads | £30,000 |

**Complete the table below to show the unit cost at the production level of 150,000 units.**

| Element | Unit cost at 150,000 units £ |
|---|---|
| Materials | |
| Labour | |
| Overheads | |
| Total | |

## Task 8

(a) **Reorder the following headings and costs into a manufacturing account format on the right side of the table below for the year ended 31 December.**

| Heading | Cost £ | Manufacturing costs | £ |
|---|---|---|---|
| Closing inventory of work in progress | 35,000 | | |
| Direct labour | 252,500 | | |
| Opening inventory of raw materials | 27,500 | | |
| Closing inventory of finished goods | 72,500 | | |
| Closing inventory of raw materials | 35,000 | | |
| Manufacturing overheads | 142,500 | | |
| COST OF GOODS SOLD | | | |
| MANUFACTURING COST | | | |
| Purchases of raw materials | 135,000 | | |
| Opening inventory of work in progress | 30,000 | | |
| Opening inventory of finished goods | 85,000 | | |
| DIRECT COST | | | |
| DIRECT MATERIALS USED | | | |
| COST OF GOODS MANUFACTURED | | | |

(b) **Enter the correct figures for the following costs which were not provided in part (a).**

| Manufacturing account | £ |
|---|---|
| DIRECT MATERIALS USED | |
| DIRECT COST | |
| MANUFACTURING COST | |
| COST OF GOODS MANUFACTURED | |
| COST OF GOODS SOLD | |

## Task 9

You are told the opening inventory of a single good for resale in the warehouse is 4,500 units at £7.00 per unit. During the month 2,600 units at £7.20 per unit are received and the following week 3,300 units are issued for sale.

**Complete the following table by inserting the cost of the issue and closing inventory valuation under each costing method (FIFO, LIFO and AVCO).**

| | FIFO £ | LIFO £ | AVCO £ |
|---|---|---|---|
| Issue | | | |
| Closing inventory | | | |

## Task 10

New Cross Ltd has the following movements in a certain type of inventory into and out of its stores for the month of August:

| DATE | RECEIPTS | | | ISSUES | |
|---|---|---|---|---|---|
| | Units | Cost £ | | Units | Cost £ |
| August 5 | 300 | 1,500 | | | |
| August 8 | 800 | 4,000 | | | |
| August 12 | 1,250 | 7,500 | | | |
| August 18 | | | | 2,100 | |
| August 25 | 1,000 | 6,000 | | | |

Complete the table below for the issue and closing inventory values.

| Method | Cost of issue on 18 August £ | Closing inventory at 31 August £ |
|---|---|---|
| FIFO | | |
| LIFO | | |
| AVCO | | |

# Task 11

(a) **From the characteristics listed, identify the labour payment method by putting a tick in the relevant column of the table below.**

| Characteristic | Time-rate | Piecework | Time-rate with overtime |
|---|---|---|---|
| Payment is made for each unit or task successfully completed | | | |
| Workers are paid a day rate based on the hours they work | | | |
| Overtime is paid for hours in excess of the basic agreed level | | | |

(b) Charing Cross Ltd pays a time-rate of £14 per hour to its direct labour for a standard 35-hour week. Any of the labour force working in excess of 35 hours is paid an overtime rate of £28 per hour.

**Calculate the gross wage for the week for the two workers in the table below.**

| Worker | Hours worked | Basic wage £ | Overtime £ | Gross wage £ |
|---|---|---|---|---|
| S Toni | 35 | | | |
| A Partridge | 39 | | | |

# Task 12

London Bridge Ltd uses a piecework method to pay labour in one of its factories. The rate used is 65p per unit produced.

**Calculate the gross wage for the week for the two workers in the table below.**

| Worker | Units produced in week | Gross wage £ |
|---|---|---|
| C Hynde | 450 | |
| D Harry | 390 | |

## Task 13

Waterloo Ltd uses a time-rate method with bonus to pay its direct labour in one of its factories. The time-rate used is £11.50 per hour and a worker is expected to produce 4 units an hour, anything over this and the worker is paid a bonus of £1.50 per unit.

**Calculate the gross wage for the week including bonus for the three workers in the table below.**

| Worker | Hours worked | Units produced | Basic wage £ | Bonus £ | Gross wage £ |
|---|---|---|---|---|---|
| M Jagger | 35 | 130 | | | |
| K Richard | 35 | 139 | | | |
| C Watts | 35 | 160 | | | |

## Task 14

Hally Ltd makes a single product and has the following production and cost data:

Variable Costs    £7.50 per unit
Fixed Costs    £12,000 per month

Hally Ltd can choose to produce 500, 2,000, 4,000 or 7,500 units over its next budget period. It wishes to identify its unit cost at each level of production.

The spreadsheet below has been partly formatted in order to provide expenditure information for the next budget period.

(a) **Complete the formatting of the spreadsheet by selecting column headings from the picklist. Complete rows 3, 4 and 5 by inserting figures in the cells, correct to two decimal places.**

| | A | B | C | D | E |
|---|---|---|---|---|---|
| 1 | Units produced | [ ▼ ] | Variable Costs £ | [ ▼ ] | Unit cost £ |
| 2 | 500 | 12,000 | 3,750 | 15,750 | 31.50 |
| 3 | | | | | |
| 4 | | | | | |
| 5 | | | | | |

**Picklist:**

Fixed Costs £
Unit cost £
Units produced
Total Costs £
Variable Costs £

...........................................................................................

(b) **Insert the formulas in the table below that you used for rows 3, 4 and 5 of column E.**

| | E |
|---|---|
| 3 | |
| 4 | |
| 5 | |

...........................................................................................

## Task 15

Listed below are four statements about spreadsheets.

**Identify the statements as being True or False by putting a tick in the relevant column of the table below.**

| Statement | True | False |
|---|---|---|
| Cells can only contain numbers or formulas, not text | | |
| A spreadsheet can be formatted to be a useful presentation of data in a formal report | | |
| Data can be input to the topmost row of an empty spreadsheet, where A, B, C etc usually appear | | |
| A spreadsheet should be password protected if the data is confidential | | |

...........................................................................................

## Task 16

(a) Croydon Ltd has produced a spreadsheet detailing budgeted and actual cost for last month.

Calculate the amount of the variance for each cost type and then determine whether it is adverse or favourable by typing F for favourable and A for adverse in the right-hand column of the table below.

| | A | B | C | D | E |
|---|---|---|---|---|---|
| 1 | Cost type | Budget £ | Actual £ | Variance £ | Adverse/Favourable (A/F) |
| 2 | Direct materials | 14,500 | 12,200 | | |
| 3 | Direct labour | 5,000 | 3,125 | | |
| 4 | Production overheads | 4,000 | 6,120 | | |
| 5 | Administration overheads | 3,000 | 4,950 | | |
| 6 | Selling and Distribution overheads | 5,000 | 2,950 | | |

(b) Insert the formulas in the table below that you used for cells 2, 3, 4, 5 and 6 of column D of the spreadsheet.

| | D |
|---|---|
| 1 | Variance £ |
| 2 | |
| 3 | |
| 4 | |
| 5 | |
| 6 | |

# Task 17

(a) **A spreadsheet has been prepared for Selworthy Ltd for last year as follows.**

| | A | B | C | D |
|---|---|---|---|---|
| 1 | Cost type | Budget £ | Variance £ | Adverse/ Favourable |
| 2 | Direct materials | 5,000 | 335 | Adverse |
| 3 | Direct labour | 7,000 | 815 | Adverse |
| 4 | Production overheads | 6,000 | 428 | Favourable |
| 5 | Administration overheads | 4,000 | 580 | Adverse |
| 6 | Selling and Distribution overheads | 2,000 | 150 | Adverse |

To re-order rows 2 to 6 of the spreadsheet so that the variances in column C are presented in descending order of size, which sort button would you use? Answer yes or no for each button by placing a tick in the relevant column.

| | Yes | No |
|---|---|---|
| A Z ↓ Sort | | |
| Z A ↓ Sort | | |

**When the rows are sorted correctly, which variance would appear in cell C4? Tick ONE box.**

| Variance £ | Appears in cell C4 |
|---|---|
| 335 | |
| 815 | |
| 428 | |
| 580 | |
| 150 | |

(b) The following spreadsheet shows budgeted costs plus variances for last month for Selworthy Ltd. It is company policy to provide managers with a variance report highlighting significant variances, which is any variance of 10% or more

**Indicate whether each variance is significant or not significant by using the picklist.**

| | A | B | C | D | E |
|---|---|---|---|---|---|
| 1 | Cost type | Budget £ | Variance £ | Adverse/ Favourable | Significa Not significa |
| 2 | Direct materials | 5,000 | 335 | Adverse | |
| 3 | Direct labour | 7,000 | 815 | Adverse | |
| 4 | Production overheads | 6,000 | 428 | Favourable | |
| 5 | Administration overheads | 4,000 | 580 | Adverse | |
| 6 | Selling and Distribution overheads | 2,000 | 150 | Adverse | |

**Picklist:**

Significant
Not significant

# BPP PRACTICE ASSESSMENT 5
# BASIC COSTING

# ANSWERS

# Basic Costing BPP practice assessment 5

## Task 1

(a)

|  | True | False |
|---|:---:|:---:|
| Fixed cost per unit rises as output in units rises |  | ✓ |
| Variable cost per unit remains constant whatever the level of output | ✓ |  |
| A business with an investment centre can code assets and liabilities for it | ✓ |  |
| Many fixed costs are only fixed over a certain range of output | ✓ |  |

(b)

| Description | Sole trader | Partnership | Limited company |
|---|:---:|:---:|:---:|
| A group of individuals who trade together intending to make a profit |  | ✓ |  |
| Shareholders own the business but it is managed by directors and managers |  |  | ✓ |
| The owner trades under their own name | ✓ |  |  |

## Task 2

(a)

| Cost | Materials | Labour | Overheads |
|---|---|---|---|
| Wages of machine operators making the chimes | | ✓ | |
| Telephone charges for workshop floor telephone | | | ✓ |
| Tin used in making the chimes | ✓ | | |
| Salary of the supervisor on the workshop floor | | | ✓ |

(b)

| Cost | Direct | Indirect |
|---|---|---|
| Buttons used on suit jackets | ✓ | |
| Rent and rates for shop and workshop | | ✓ |
| Licences paid to designers each time a suit pattern is used | ✓ | |
| Oil for sewing machines | | ✓ |

## Task 3

(a)

| Cost | Production | Administration | Financing |
|---|---|---|---|
| Cogs used in timing movements | ✓ | | |
| Wages of payroll staff | | ✓ | |
| Overdraft charges | | | ✓ |
| Salaries of clockmakers | ✓ | | |

(b)

| Cost | Fixed | Variable | Semi-variable |
|---|---|---|---|
| Spun fibre used in making the panels | | ✓ | |
| Salary of supervisor on the factory floor | ✓ | | |
| Electricity costs for the machines that include a standing charge | | | ✓ |
| Labour costs paid on a piecework basis | | ✓ | |

## Task 4

| Transaction | Code |
|---|---|
| Telephone charges for the payroll department | 05/200 |
| Factory rates | 03/200 |
| Sales to Japan | 01/200 |
| Sales to Greater Manchester | 01/100 |
| Material for toys | 03/100 |
| Petrol for sales vans | 07/200 |

## Task 5

| Cost | Code |
|---|---|
| Wages of spa therapists | B100 |
| Fees for designer creating new website for spa | C200 |
| Spa salts and minerals used in treatments | A100 |
| Cleaning materials used by cleaners at the spa | A200 |
| Maintenance staff wages | B200 |

# Task 6

(a)

| Statement | Fixed | Variable | Semi-variable |
|---|:---:|:---:|:---:|
| Costs of £72,000 are made up of a fixed charge of £23,000 and a further cost of £0.70 per unit at 70,000 units | | | ✓ |
| Costs of £1.80 per unit at 5,300 units and £1.06 per unit at 9,000 units | ✓ | | |
| Costs are £25,000 units at 10,000 units and £40,000 at 16,000 units | | ✓ | |

**Workings:**

2   5,300 × £1.80 = £9,540; 9,000 × £1.06 = £9,540. Therefore this is a fixed cost

3   £25,000/10,000 = £2.50 per unit; £40,000/16,000 = £2.50 per unit. Therefore this is a variable cost

(b)

| Costs | Fixed | Variable |
|---|:---:|:---:|
| Cost of ink used in a printing press | | ✓ |
| Straight-line depreciation on plant and machinery | ✓ | |
| Salary of supervisor | ✓ | |
| Timber for making chairs in furniture factory | | ✓ |

# Task 7

(a)

| Element | Total cost at 13,000 units £ | Unit cost at 13,000 units £ |
|---|---|---|
| Materials | 97,500 | 7.50 |
| Labour | 71,500 | 5.50 |
| Overheads | 130,000 | 10.00 |
| Total | 299,000 | 23.00 |

(b)

| Element | Unit cost at 150,000 units £ |
|---|---|
| Materials | 1.00 |
| Labour | 0.75 |
| Overheads | 0.20 |
| Total | 1.95 |

# Task 8

(a)

**Manufacturing Account    Y/e 31 December**

|  | £ |
|---|---|
| Opening inventory of raw materials | 27,500 |
| Purchases of raw materials | 135,000 |
| Closing inventory of raw materials | 35,000 |
| DIRECT MATERIALS USED |  |
| Direct labour | 252,500 |
| DIRECT COST |  |
| Manufacturing overheads | 142,500 |
| MANUFACTURING COST |  |
| Opening inventory of work in progress | 30,000 |
| Closing inventory of work in progress | 35,000 |
| COST OF GOODS MANUFACTURED |  |
| Opening inventory of finished goods | 85,000 |
| Closing inventory of finished goods | 72,500 |
| COST OF GOODS SOLD |  |

(b)

| Manufacturing account | £ |
|---|---|
| DIRECT MATERIALS USED | 127,500 |
| DIRECT COST | 380,000 |
| MANUFACTURING COST | 522,500 |
| COST OF GOODS MANUFACTURED | 517,500 |
| COST OF GOODS SOLD | 530,000 |

## Task 9

|  | FIFO £ | LIFO £ | AVCO £ |
|---|---|---|---|
| Issue | 23,100 | 23,620 | 23,342 |
| Closing inventory | 27,120 | 26,600 | 26,878 |

**Workings:**

|  | Units | Per unit £ | Total £ | Balance £ |
|---|---|---|---|---|
| Opening inventory | 4,500 | 7.00 | 31,500 | 31,500 |
| Received | 2,600 | 7.20 | 18,720 | 50,220 |
|  | 7,100 |  |  |  |
| Issued | (3,300) |  |  |  |
| Closing inventory | 3,800 |  |  |  |

|  | FIFO | LIFO | AVCO |
|---|---|---|---|
| Issue | 3,300 × £7 = £23,100 | £18,720 + (700 × £7) = £23,620 | 3,300 × £50,220/7,100 = £23,342 |
| Closing inventory | (1,200 × £7) + £18,720 = £27,120 | 3,800 × £7= £26,600 | 3,800 × £50,220/7,100 = £26,878 |

---

## Task 10

| Method | Cost of issue on 18 August £ | Closing inventory at 31 August £ |
|---|---|---|
| FIFO | (1,500 + 4,000 + (1,000/1,250 × 7,500)) = **£11,500** | (250/1,250 × 7,500) + 6,000 = **£7,500** |
| LIFO | (7,500 + 4,000 + (50/300 × 1,500)) = **£11,750** | (6,000 +(250/300 × 1,500)) = **£7,250** |
| AVCO | (2,100/2,350 × 13,000) = **£11,617** | (6,000 + (250/2,350 × 13,000)) = **£7,383** |

---

BPP
LEARNING MEDIA

# Task 11

(a)

| Characteristic | Time-rate | Piecework | Time-rate with overtime |
|---|---|---|---|
| Payment is made for each unit or task successfully completed | | ✓ | |
| Workers are paid a day rate based on the hours they work | ✓ | | |
| Overtime is paid for hours in excess of the basic agreed level | | | ✓ |

(b)

| Worker | Hours worked | Basic wage £ | Overtime £ | Gross wage £ |
|---|---|---|---|---|
| S Toni | 35 hours | 490 | 0 | 490 |
| A Partridge | 39 hours | 490 | 112 | 602 |

# Task 12

| Worker | Units produced in week | Gross wage £ |
|---|---|---|
| C Hynde | 450 | 292.50 |
| D Harry | 390 | 253.50 |

# Task 13

| Worker | Hours worked | Units produced | Basic wage £ | Bonus £ | Gross wage £ |
|---|---|---|---|---|---|
| M Jagger | 35 | 130 | 402.50 | 0 | 402.50 |
| K Richard | 35 | 139 | 402.50 | 0 | 402.50 |
| C Watts | 35 | 160 | 402.50 | 30 | 432.50 |

# Task 14

(a)

|  | A | B | C | D | E |
|---|---|---|---|---|---|
| 1 | Units produced | Fixed costs £ | Variable Costs £ | Total costs £ | Unit cost £ |
| 2 | 500 | 12,000 | 3,750 | 15,750 | 31.50 |
| 3 | 2,000 | 12,000 | 15,000 | 27,000 | 13.50 |
| 4 | 4,000 | 12,000 | 30,000 | 42,000 | 10.50 |
| 5 | 7,500 | 12,000 | 56,250 | 68,250 | 9.10 |

(b)

|  | E |
|---|---|
| 3 | =(D3/A3) |
| 4 | =(D4/A4) |
| 5 | =(D5/A5) |

# Task 15

| Statement | True | False |
|---|---|---|
| Cells can only contain numbers or formulas, not text | | ✓ |
| A spreadsheet can be formatted to be a useful presentation of data in a formal report | ✓ | |
| Data can be input to the topmost row of an empty spreadsheet, where A, B, C etc usually appear | | ✓ |
| A spreadsheet should be password protected if the data is confidential | ✓ | |

# Task 16

(a)

| | A | B | C | D | E |
|---|---|---|---|---|---|
| 1 | Cost type | Budget £ | Actual £ | Variance £ | Adverse/Favourable (A/F) |
| 2 | Direct materials | 14,500 | 12,200 | 2,300 | F |
| 3 | Direct labour | 5,000 | 3,125 | 1,875 | F |
| 4 | Production overheads | 4,000 | 6,120 | 2,120 | A |
| 5 | Administration overheads | 3,000 | 4,950 | 1,950 | A |
| 6 | Selling and Distribution overheads | 5,000 | 2,950 | 2,050 | F |

(b)

| | D |
|---|---|
| 1 | Variance £ |
| 2 | =(B2-C2) |
| 3 | =(B3-C3) |
| 4 | =(B4-C4) |
| 5 | =(B5-C5) |
| 6 | =(B6-C6) |

# Task 17

(a)

|  | Yes | No |
|---|---|---|
| A Z ↓ Sort |  | ✓ |
| Z A ↓ Sort | ✓ |  |

| Variance £ | Appears in cell C4 |
|---|---|
| 335 |  |
| 815 |  |
| 428 | ✓ |
| 580 |  |
| 150 |  |

(b)

|  | A | B | C | D | E |
|---|---|---|---|---|---|
| 1 | Cost type | Budget £ | Variance £ | Adverse/ Favourable | Significant/ Not significant |
| 2 | Direct materials | 5,000 | 335 | Adverse | Not significant |
| 3 | Direct labour | 7,000 | 815 | Adverse | Significant |
| 4 | Production overheads | 6,000 | 428 | Favourable | Not significant |
| 5 | Administration overheads | 4,000 | 580 | Adverse | Significant |
| 6 | Selling and Distribution overheads | 2,000 | 150 | Adverse | Not significant |

# BPP PRACTICE ASSESSMENT 6
# BASIC COSTING

**Time allowed: 2 hours**

PRACTICE ASSESSMENT 6

# Basic Costing BPP practice assessment 6

## Task 1

(a) **Identify the following statements as True or False by putting a tick in the relevant column of the table below.**

|  | True | False |
|---|---|---|
| The fixed cost per unit rises over the level of output |  |  |
| The variable cost per unit falls over the level of output |  |  |
| LIFO gives the lowest value of closing inventory if prices are rising |  |  |
| An investment centre can have capital amounts coded to it |  |  |

(b) **Read the descriptions below and match them to the type of system by putting a tick in the correct box.**

| Description | Management accounting | Financial accounting |
|---|---|---|
| Purchase invoices are entered into the purchases day book |  |  |
| Invoices are analysed to determine whether they are materials or expenses |  |  |
| The costs on the invoice are added to costs already collected for a cost centre |  |  |
| Individual invoices are posted to creditor accounts |  |  |

## Task 2

(a)  Hawes Ltd makes goats' cheese in its creamery.

**Classify the following costs by element (materials, labour or overheads) by putting a tick in the relevant column of the table below.**

| Cost | Materials | Labour | Overheads |
|---|---|---|---|
| Milk from goats delivered to the creamery | | | |
| Electricity charges for offices | | | |
| Wages of workers employed to churn the cheese | | | |
| Salary of the supervisor on the workshop floor | | | |

(b)  Kilnsey Ltd is in business as a walking boot shop selling boots and making repairs.

**Classify the following costs by nature (direct or indirect) by putting a tick in the relevant column of the table below.**

| Cost | Direct | Indirect |
|---|---|---|
| Wages of cobbler employed to repair the boots | | |
| Rent and rates for shop and workshop | | |
| Licences paid per item to boot suppliers to stock their boots | | |
| Oil for stitching machine | | |

## Task 3

(a) Pateley Ltd makes fishing rods.

**Classify the following costs by function (production, administration, or financing) by putting a tick in the relevant column of the table below.**

| Cost | Production | Administration | Financing |
|---|---|---|---|
| Nylon line used in the rods | | | |
| Wages of manager's secretary | | | |
| Loan interest paid yearly | | | |
| Salary of employee making the fishing rods | | | |

(b) Blubberhouses Ltd smokes fish and beef for sale.

**Classify the following costs by their behaviour (fixed, variable, or semi-variable) by putting a tick in the relevant column of the table below.**

| Cost | Fixed | Variable | Semi-variable |
|---|---|---|---|
| Smoking of salmon fillets | | | |
| Salary of supervisor on the workshop floor | | | |
| Gas costs for the smoking machines that include a standing charge | | | |
| Basic element of labour costs paid on a time-rate basis | | | |

## Task 4

Dales Limited operates a restaurant and uses a numeric coding system for its elements of cost (materials, labour or overheads) and then further classifies each element by nature (direct or indirect cost) as below. So, for example, the code for direct materials is 50100.

| Element of cost | Code | Nature of cost | Code |
|---|---|---|---|
| Materials | 50 | Direct | 100 |
| | | Indirect | 200 |
| Labour | 60 | Direct | 100 |
| | | Indirect | 200 |
| Overheads | 70 | Direct | 100 |
| | | Indirect | 200 |

**Code the following costs, extracted from invoices and payroll, using the table below.**

| Cost | Code |
|---|---|
| Solicitor fees for arranging restaurant licence | |
| Fresh vegetables bought in daily from local farmers | |
| Waiting staff salaries | |
| Cleaning materials used by restaurant cleaners | |
| Security manager salary | |

## Task 5

Birstwith Ltd makes dog accessories. It uses an alpha-numerical coding structure based on one profit centre and three cost centres as outlined below. Each code has a three digit sub-code so each transaction will be coded as *****.

| Profit/Cost centre | Code | Sub-classification | Sub-code |
|---|---|---|---|
| Sales | SA | UK sales | 100 |
| | | Overseas sales | 200 |
| Production | PD | Direct cost | 100 |
| | | Indirect cost | 200 |
| Administration | AD | Direct cost | 100 |
| | | Indirect cost | 200 |
| Selling and Distribution | SD | Direct cost | 100 |
| | | Indirect cost | 200 |

**Code the following revenue and expense transactions using the table below.**

| Transaction | Code |
|---|---|
| Telephone charges for the payroll department | |
| Factory business rates | |
| Sales to the USA | |
| Sales to London | |
| Material for dog blankets | |
| Salary of sales representative | |

BPP
LEARNING MEDIA

## Task 6

(a) **Identify the following statements as either True or False by putting a tick in the relevant column of the table below.**

|  | True | False |
|---|---|---|
| Step fixed costs show a sudden jump in cost to a new level when expansion goes beyond a certain level |  |  |
| With variable costs each unit of output causes the same amount of cost to be incurred |  |  |
| Direct costs are generally fixed |  |  |

(b) **Classify the following costs as either fixed or variable by putting a tick in the relevant column of the table below.**

| Costs | Fixed | Variable |
|---|---|---|
| Fees for bookkeeper to write up accounts |  |  |
| Glue for repairing books |  |  |
| Salary of supervisor in warehouse |  |  |
| Cake mix for wedding cake production line in bakery |  |  |

## Task 7

(a) Burnsall Ltd is costing a single product, which has the following cost details:

Variable costs per unit

| | |
|---|---|
| Materials | £10.50 |
| Labour | £12.45 |

| | |
|---|---|
| Total overheads | £13,000 |

**Complete the following total cost and unit cost table for a production level of 13,000 units.**

| Element | Total cost at 13,000 units £ | Unit cost at 13,000 units £ |
|---|---|---|
| Materials | | |
| Labour | | |
| Overheads | | |
| Total | | |

(b) Skipton Ltd makes a single product and for a production level of 12,000 units has the following cost details:

| | |
|---|---|
| Materials 3,000 kilos at | £10 per kilo |
| Labour 4,000 hours at | £15 an hour |
| Overheads | £30,000 |

**Complete the table below to show the unit cost at the production level of 12,000 units.**

| Element | Unit cost at 12,000 units £ |
|---|---|
| Materials | |
| Labour | |
| Overheads | |
| Total | |

## Task 8

(a) **Reorder the following headings and costs into a manufacturing account format on the right side of the table below for the year ended 31 December.**

| Heading | Cost £'000 | Manufacturing account | £'000 |
|---|---|---|---|
| Closing inventory of work in progress | 8,300 | | |
| Direct labour | 12,800 | | |
| Opening inventory of raw materials | 7,500 | | |
| Closing inventory of finished goods | 45,700 | | |
| Closing inventory of raw materials | 5,600 | | |
| Manufacturing overheads | 10,250 | | |
| COST OF GOODS SOLD | | | |
| MANUFACTURING COST | | | |
| Purchases of raw materials | 13,000 | | |
| Opening inventory of work in progress | 9,850 | | |
| Opening inventory of finished goods | 44,600 | | |
| DIRECT COST | | | |
| DIRECT MATERIALS USED | | | |
| COST OF GOODS MANUFACTURED | | | |

(b) **Enter the correct figures for the following costs which were not provided in part (a).**

| Manufacturing account | £ |
|---|---|
| DIRECT MATERIALS USED | |
| DIRECT COST | |
| MANUFACTURING COST | |
| COST OF GOODS MANUFACTURED | |
| COST OF GOODS SOLD | |

## Task 9

You are told the opening inventory of a single good for resale in the warehouse is 6,300 units at £2.70 per unit. During the month 5,100 units at £2.80 per unit are received and the following week 9,600 units are issued for sale.

**Complete the following table by inserting the cost of the issue and closing inventory valuation under each costing method (FIFO, LIFO and AVCO).**

| | FIFO £ | LIFO £ | AVCO £ |
|---|---|---|---|
| Issue | | | |
| Closing inventory | | | |

## Task 10

Ripon Ltd has the following movements in a certain type of inventory into and out of its stores for the month of October:

| DATE | RECEIPTS | | | ISSUES | |
|---|---|---|---|---|---|
| | Units | Cost £ | | Units | Cost £ |
| October 5 | 300 | 900 | | | |
| October 8 | 600 | 2,400 | | | |
| October 12 | 500 | 2,500 | | | |
| October 18 | | | | 1,200 | |
| October 25 | 1,000 | 6,000 | | | |

Complete the table below for the issue and closing inventory values.

| Method | Cost of issue on 18 October £ | Closing inventory at 31 October £ |
|---|---|---|
| FIFO | | |
| LIFO | | |
| AVCO | | |

····································································································

## Task 11

(a) **For each of the following characteristics, identify the labour payment method by putting a tick in the relevant column of the table below.**

| Characteristic | Time-rate | Piecework | Piecework plus bonus |
|---|---|---|---|
| Workers paid under this method are encouraged to produce more at all levels of activity | | | |
| A basic amount is paid per hour worked | | | |
| A bonus is paid for output in excess of that expected | | | |

····································································································

(b) Settle Ltd pays a time-rate of £10 per hour to its direct labour for a standard 37.5-hour week. Any of the labour force working in excess of 37.5 hours is paid an overtime rate of £12 per hour.

**Calculate the gross wage for the week for the two workers in the table below.**

| Worker | Hours worked | Basic wage £ | Overtime £ | Gross wage £ |
|--------|--------------|--------------|------------|--------------|
| N Crane | 37.5 | | | |
| F Crane | 39 | | | |

## Task 12

Leyburn Ltd uses a piecework method to pay labour in one of its factories. The rate used is 95p per unit produced.

**Calculate the gross wage for the week for the two workers in the table below.**

| Worker | Units produced in week | Gross wage £ |
|--------|------------------------|--------------|
| P Freire | 925 | |
| J Rousseau | 870 | |

## Task 13

Richmond Ltd uses a time-rate method with bonus to pay its direct labour in one of its factories. The time-rate used is £9.75 per hour and a worker is expected to produce five units an hour, anything over this and the worker is paid a bonus of £1.50 per unit.

**Calculate the gross wage for the week including bonus for the three workers in the table below.**

| Worker | Hours worked | Units produced | Basic wage £ | Bonus £ | Gross wage £ |
|--------|--------------|----------------|--------------|---------|--------------|
| U Bolt | 35 | 175 | | | |
| C Ohuruogu | 35 | 205 | | | |
| S Coe | 35 | 210 | | | |

## Task 14

Paige Ltd makes a single product and has the following production and cost data:

Variable Costs     £3.50 per unit
Fixed Costs        £8,800 per month

Paige Ltd can choose to produce 1,000, 2,000, 3,000 or 4,000 units over its next budget period. It wishes to identify its unit cost at each level of production.

The spreadsheet below has been partly formatted in order to provide expenditure information for the three months.

(a) **Complete the formatting of the spreadsheet by selecting column headings from the picklist. Complete rows 3, 4 and 5 by inserting figures in the cells, correct to two decimal places.**

|   | A | B | C | D | E |
|---|---|---|---|---|---|
| 1 | Units produced | ▼ | ▼ | Total costs £ | Unit cost £ |
| 2 | 1,000 | 8,800 | 3,500 | 12,300 | 12.30 |
| 3 |  |  |  |  |  |
| 4 |  |  |  |  |  |
| 5 |  |  |  |  |  |

**Picklist:**

Fixed Costs £
Unit cost £
Units produced
Total Costs £
Variable Costs £

. . . . . . . . . . . . . . . . . . . . . . . . . . . . . . . . . . . . . . . . . . . . . . . . . . . . . . . . . . . . . . . . . . . . . . . . . . . . . . . . . . . . . . . . . . . . . . . . . . . . .

(b) **Insert the formulas in the table below that you used for rows 3, 4 and 5 of column E.**

|   | E |
|---|---|
| 3 |  |
| 4 |  |
| 5 |  |

. . . . . . . . . . . . . . . . . . . . . . . . . . . . . . . . . . . . . . . . . . . . . . . . . . . . . . . . . . . . . . . . . . . . . . . . . . . . . . . . . . . . . . . . . . . . . . . . . . . . .

## Task 15

Listed below are four statements about spreadsheets.

**Identify the statements as being true or false by putting a tick in the relevant column of the table below.**

| Statement | True | False |
|---|---|---|
| The autosum formula can only add figures in a column, not in a row | | |
| There can be numerous spreadsheets in a single worksheet | | |
| Cell references in spreadsheet formulas should always be contained within brackets | | |
| Backups are not necessary for spreadsheets | | |

## Task 16

(a) Masham Ltd has the following actual results for the month of July which are to be compared to the budget:

| | |
|---|---|
| Income | £499,800 |

Expenditure:

| | |
|---|---|
| Direct materials | £156,420 |
| Direct labour | £193,750 |
| Production overheads | £24,630 |

**Enter the above data into the spreadsheet below, calculate the amount of each variance and then determine whether it is adverse or favourable by typing F for favourable and A for adverse in the right-hand column of the table below.**

| | A | B | C | D | E |
|---|---|---|---|---|---|
| 1 | Cost type | Budget £ | Actual £ | Variance £ | Adverse (A)/ Favourable (F) |
| 2 | Income | 504,000 | | | |
| 3 | Direct materials | 158,000 | | | |
| 4 | Direct labour | 189,000 | | | |
| 5 | Production overheads | 26,000 | | | |

(b) **Insert the formulas in the table below that you used for cells 2, 3, 4 and 5 of <u>column D</u> of the spreadsheet.**

|   | D |
|---|---|
| 1 | Variance £ |
| 2 | |
| 3 | |
| 4 | |
| 5 | |

## Task 17

(a) The following performance report for this month has been produced for Catterick Ltd as summarised in the spreadsheet below. Any variance in excess of 10% of budget is deemed to be significant and should be reported to the relevant manager for review and appropriate action.

**Examine the variances in the spreadsheet below and indicate whether they are significant or not significant by typing S for significant and NS for not significant in the right-hand column below.**

|   | A | B | C | D | E |
|---|---|---|---|---|---|
| 1 | Cost type | Budget £ | Variance £ | Adverse/ Favourable | Significant/ Not significant |
| 2 | Direct materials | 45,000 | 335 | Adverse | |
| 3 | Direct labour | 27,000 | 815 | Adverse | |
| 4 | Production overheads | 16,000 | 2,428 | Favourable | |
| 5 | Administration overheads | 14,000 | 580 | Adverse | |
| 6 | Selling and Distribution overheads | 12,000 | 1,500 | Adverse | |

(b) Catterick Ltd is considering including the calculation involved in determining whether a variance is significant in a separate column in the spreadsheet.

**Which of the following formulas for row 4 is appropriate for identifying whether the production overhead variance is significant? Tick one item.**

| Formula | Appropriate for calculating significance of production overhead variance |
|---|---|
| =(C4*B4) | |
| =AVERAGE(C4:B4) | |
| =SUM(C4:B4) | |
| =(C4/B4) | |

# BPP PRACTICE ASSESSMENT 6
# BASIC COSTING

# ANSWERS

# Basic Costing BPP practice assessment 6

## Task 1

(a)

|  | True | False |
|---|---|---|
| The fixed cost per unit rises over the level of output |  | ✓ |
| The variable cost per unit falls over the level of output |  | ✓ |
| LIFO gives the lowest value of closing inventory if prices are rising | ✓ |  |
| An investment centre can have capital amounts coded to it | ✓ |  |

(b)

| Description | Management accounting | Financial accounting |
|---|---|---|
| Purchase invoices are entered into the purchases day book |  | ✓ |
| Invoices are analysed to determine whether they are materials or expenses | ✓ |  |
| The costs on the invoice are added to costs already collected for a cost centre | ✓ |  |
| Individual invoices are posted to creditor accounts |  | ✓ |

## Task 2

(a)

| Cost | Materials | Labour | Overheads |
|---|---|---|---|
| Milk from goats delivered to the creamery | ✓ | | |
| Electricity charges for offices | | | ✓ |
| Wages of workers employed to churn the cheese | | ✓ | |
| Salary of the supervisor on the workshop floor | | | ✓ |

(b)

| Cost | Direct | Indirect |
|---|---|---|
| Wages of cobbler employed to repair the boots | ✓ | |
| Rent and rates for shop and workshop | | ✓ |
| Licences paid per item to boot suppliers to stock their boots | ✓ | |
| Oil for stitching machine | | ✓ |

## Task 3

(a)

| Cost | Production | Administration | Financing |
|---|---|---|---|
| Nylon line used in the rods | ✓ | | |
| Wages of manager's secretary | | ✓ | |
| Loan interest paid yearly | | | ✓ |
| Salary of employee making the fishing rods | ✓ | | |

(b)

| Cost | Fixed | Variable | Semi-variable |
|------|-------|----------|---------------|
| Smoking of salmon fillets | | ✓ | |
| Salary of supervisor on the workshop floor | ✓ | | |
| Gas costs for the smoking machines that include a standing charge | | | ✓ |
| Basic element of labour costs paid on a time-rate basis | ✓ | | |

## Task 4

| Cost | Code |
|------|------|
| Solicitor fees for arranging restaurant licence | 70200 |
| Fresh vegetables bought in daily from local farmers | 50100 |
| Waiting staff salaries | 60100 |
| Cleaning materials used by restaurant cleaners | 50200 |
| Security manager salary | 60200 |

## Task 5

| Transaction | Code |
|-------------|------|
| Telephone charges for the payroll department | AD200 |
| Factory business rates | PD200 |
| Sales to the USA | SA200 |
| Sales to London | SA100 |
| Material for dog blankets | PD100 |
| Salary of sales representative | SD200 |

# Task 6

## (a)

|  | True | False |
|---|---|---|
| Step fixed costs show a sudden jump in cost to a new level when expansion goes beyond a certain level | ✓ |  |
| With variable costs each unit of output causes the same amount of cost to be incurred | ✓ |  |
| Direct costs are generally fixed |  | ✓ |

## (b)

| Costs | Fixed | Variable |
|---|---|---|
| Fees for bookkeeper to write-up accounts | ✓ |  |
| Glue for repairing books |  | ✓ |
| Salary of supervisor in warehouse | ✓ |  |
| Cake mix for wedding cake production line in bakery |  | ✓ |

# Task 7

## (a)

| Element | Total cost at 13,000 units £ | Unit cost at 13,000 units £ |
|---|---|---|
| Materials | 136,500 | 10.50 |
| Labour | 161,850 | 12.45 |
| Overheads | 13,000 | 1.00 |
| Total | 311,350 | 23.95 |

(b)

| Element | Unit cost at 12,000 units £ |
|---------|------------------------------|
| Materials | 2.50 |
| Labour | 5.00 |
| Overheads | 2.50 |
| Total | 10.00 |

# Task 8

## (a) Manufacturing Account Y/e 31 December

| Heading | Cost £'000 | | £'000 |
|---|---|---|---|
| Closing inventory of work in progress | 8,300 | Opening inventory of raw materials | 7,500 |
| Direct labour | 12,800 | Purchases of raw materials | 13,000 |
| Opening inventory of raw materials | 7,500 | Closing inventory of raw materials | 5,600 |
| Closing inventory of finished goods | 45,700 | DIRECT MATERIALS USED | |
| Closing inventory of raw materials | 5,600 | Direct labour | 12,800 |
| Manufacturing overheads | 10,250 | DIRECT COST | |
| COST OF GOODS SOLD | | Manufacturing Overheads | 10,250 |
| MANUFACTURING COST | | MANUFACTURING COST | |
| Purchases of raw materials | 13,000 | Opening inventory of work in progress | 9,850 |
| Opening inventory of work in progress | 9,850 | Closing inventory of work in progress | 8,300 |
| Opening inventory of finished goods | 44,600 | COST OF GOODS MANUFACTURED | |
| DIRECT COST | | Opening inventory of finished goods | 44,600 |
| DIRECT MATERIALS USED | | Closing inventory of finished goods | 45,700 |
| COST OF GOODS MANUFACTURED | | COST OF GOODS SOLD | |

(b)

| Manufacturing account | £ |
|---|---|
| DIRECT MATERIALS USED | 14,900 |
| DIRECT COST | 27,700 |
| MANUFACTURING COST | 37,950 |
| COST OF GOODS MANUFACTURED | 39,500 |
| COST OF GOODS SOLD | 38,400 |

## Task 9

| | FIFO £ | LIFO £ | AVCO £ |
|---|---|---|---|
| Issue | 26,250 | 26,430 | 26,349 |
| Closing inventory | 5,040 | 4,860 | 4,941 |

**Workings:**

| | Units | Per unit £ | Total £ | Balance £ |
|---|---|---|---|---|
| Opening inventory | 6,300 | 2.70 | 17,010 | 17,010 |
| Received | 5,100 | 2.80 | 14,280 | 31,290 |
| | 11,400 | | | |
| Issued | (9,600) | | | |
| Closing inventory | 1,800 | | | |

| | FIFO | LIFO | AVCO |
|---|---|---|---|
| Issue | £17,010 + (3,300 × £2.80) = £26,250 | £14,280 + (4,500 × £2.70) = £26,430 | 9,600 × £31,290/11,400 = £26,349 |
| Closing inventory | 1,800 × £2.80 = £5,040 | 1,800 × £2.70 = £4,860 | 1,800 × £31,290/11,400 = £4,941 |

# Task 10

| Method | Cost of issue on 18 October £ | Closing inventory at 31 October £ |
|---|---|---|
| FIFO | (900 + 2,400 + (300/500 × 2,500)) = **£4,800** | (6,000 + (200/500 × 2,500)) = **£7,000** |
| LIFO | (2,500 + 2,400 + (100/300 × 900)) = **£5,200** | (6,000 + (200/300 × 900)) = **£6,600** |
| AVCO | (1,200/1,400 × 5,800) = **£4,971** | (6,000 + (200/1,400 × 5,800)) = **£6,829** |

# Task 11

(a)

| Payment method | Time-rate | Piecework | Piecework plus bonus |
|---|---|---|---|
| Workers paid under this method are encouraged to produce more at all levels of activity | | ✓ | |
| A basic amount is paid per hour worked | ✓ | | |
| A bonus is paid for output in excess of that expected | | | ✓ |

(b)

| Worker | Hours worked | Basic wage £ | Overtime £ | Gross wage £ |
|---|---|---|---|---|
| N Crane | 37.5 | 375.00 | 0 | 375.00 |
| F Crane | 39 | 375.00 | 18.00 | 393.00 |

# Task 12

| Worker | Units produced in week | Gross wage £ |
|---|---|---|
| P Freire | 925 | 878.75 |
| J Rousseau | 870 | 826.50 |

# Task 13

| Worker | Hours worked | Units produced | Basic wage £ | Bonus £ | Gross wage £ |
|---|---|---|---|---|---|
| U Bolt | 35 | 175 | 341.25 | 0 | 341.25 |
| S Ohuruogu | 35 | 205 | 341.25 | 45.00 | 386.25 |
| S Coe | 35 | 210 | 341.25 | 52.50 | 393.75 |

# Task 14

(a)

| | A | B | C | D | E |
|---|---|---|---|---|---|
| 1 | Units produced | Fixed costs £ | Variable costs £ | Total costs £ | Unit cost £ |
| 2 | 1,000 | 8,800 | 3,500 | 12,300 | 12.30 |
| 3 | 2,000 | 8,800 | 7,000 | 15,800 | 7.90 |
| 4 | 3,000 | 8,800 | 10,500 | 19,300 | 6.43 |
| 5 | 4,000 | 8,800 | 14,000 | 22,800 | 5.70 |

(b) **Insert the formulas in the table below that you used for rows 3, 4 and 5 of column E.**

| | E |
|---|---|
| 3 | =(D3/A3) |
| 4 | =(D4/A4) |
| 5 | =(D5/A5) |

## Task 15

| Statement | True | False |
|---|---|---|
| The autosum formula can only add figures in a column, not in a row | | ✓ |
| There can be numerous spreadsheets in a single worksheet | | ✓ |
| Cell references in spreadsheet formulas should always be contained within brackets | ✓ | |
| Backups are not necessary for spreadsheets | | ✓ |

## Task 16

(a)

| | A | B | C | D | E |
|---|---|---|---|---|---|
| 1 | Cost type | Budget £ | Actual £ | Variance £ | Adverse (A)/ Favourable (F) |
| 2 | Income | 504,000 | 499,800 | 4,200 | A |
| 3 | Direct materials | 158,000 | 156,420 | 1,580 | F |
| 4 | Direct labour | 189,000 | 193,750 | 4,750 | A |
| 5 | Production overheads | 26,000 | 24,630 | 1,370 | F |

(b)

| | D |
|---|---|
| 1 | Variance £ |
| 2 | =(B2-C2) |
| 3 | =(B3-C3) |
| 4 | =(B4-C4) |
| 5 | =(B5-C5) |

# Task 17

(a)

| | A | B | C | D | E |
|---|---|---|---|---|---|
| 1 | Cost type | Budget £ | Variance £ | Adverse/ Favourable | Significant/ Not significant |
| 2 | Direct materials | 45,000 | 335 | Adverse | NS |
| 3 | Direct labour | 27,000 | 815 | Adverse | NS |
| 4 | Production overheads | 16,000 | 2,428 | Favourable | S |
| 5 | Administration overheads | 14,000 | 580 | Adverse | NS |
| 6 | Selling and Distribution overheads | 12,000 | 1,500 | Adverse | S |

(b)

| Formula | Appropriate for calculating significance of production overhead variance |
|---|---|
| =(C4*B4) | |
| =AVERAGE(C4:B4) | |
| =SUM(C4:B4) | |
| =(C4/B4) | ✓ |

**Notes**

**Notes**

**Notes**

**Notes**

**Notes**

**Notes**

**Notes**